T0158281

ON OUR WAY HOME FROM THE REVOLUTION

21st CENTURY ESSAYS
David Lazar and Patrick Madden, Series Editors

ON OUR WAY HOME FROM THE REVOLUTION

REFLECTIONS ON UKRAINE

Sonya Bilocerkowycz

MAD CREEK BOOKS, AN IMPRINT OF
THE OHIO STATE UNIVERSITY PRESS
COLUMBUS

Published by Mad Creek Books, an imprint of The Ohio State University Press.

Library of Congress Cataloging-in-Publication Data
Names: Bilocerkowycz, Sonya, author.
Title: On our way home from the revolution : reflections on Ukraine / Sonya
    Bilocerkowycz.
Other titles: 21st century essays.
Description: Columbus : Mad Creek Books, an imprint of The Ohio State University
    Press, [2019] | Series: 21st century essays | Includes bibliographical references.
Identifiers: LCCN 2019010847 | ISBN 9780814255438 (pbk. ; alk. paper) | ISBN
    0814255434 (pbk. ; alk. paper)
Subjects: LCSH: Ukraine—Social conditions—1991– | Ukraine—Politics and
    government—1991– | Ukrainian diaspora.
Classification: LCC PS3602.I47 O5 2019 | DDC 814/.6—dc23
LC record available at https://lccn.loc.gov/2019010847

Cover design by Nathan Putens
Text design by Juliet Williams
Type set in Adobe Minion Pro and Fairview

For Nina

CONTENTS

NOTE ON THE TEXT

For names of cities or regions with more daily speakers of Russian, I have tended to use the Russian transliterations. For areas with more daily speakers of Ukrainian, I use the Ukrainian transliterations. With regard to Kyiv, Ukraine's capital, I use the Ukrainian transliteration at the request of the Ukrainian government. Kyiv is also the version used by the narrator's family, and that context is important for telling this particular story.

Certain words, such as *Banderites,* switch transliteration, depending on which character is using the term. And certain characters switch between Ukrainian and Russian, sometimes within the same sentence.

These are not oversights in the text, but reflections of a complex linguistic reality.

THE VILLAGE (FUGUE)

On the day of his arrest, the village elder knows many things. He knows, for example, about a milk churn buried on the edge of the forest. Inside, partisans have hidden a ledger with the names of victims. *I . . . v . . . a . . . n . . .* The ledger is a way of saying hello to those who come after. He knows about the milk churn, though he does not know it will take 73 years before it mushrooms up and out toward the light, its names soggy but intact. The village elder knows the forest and ravines are yawning, good for secrets. What the village elder does not know is that the Bolsheviks are on their way now.

The village elder knows his village is special because of the river, where peasants bathe on warm days. It is called Ikva, which sounds like a hiccup, like something caught in our throat. We meet lovers down by the river. We catch kindly water bugs. The Ikva meanders, forth and back, like the village itself. In seven years' time, we are Polish, Soviet, German, and—soon, very soon, though the village elder does not know this—we will be Soviet again. We are always, also, Ukrainian. The river runs like we do.

1

The road into the village is lined with poppies. Later, these will become a symbol of the war, but the elder will not be around to learn this fact. So for now, they are just poppies. In the village there are wheat fields out every window. Stars for a roof. Storks watching from trees.

On the day of his arrest, the village elder can account for his family. He knows that his oldest son is in the next town over attending university. This oldest son studies agriculture, our earthly things. The younger son must be out riding horses on a day like this, sunlit, blue sky, oh my. The daughters are picking greens, tending potatoes, teasing this year's pig with leftover beet stalks. Or, maybe, the daughters are down the road buying sugar and thread. In the cellar, mother is stuffing last year's pig into jars with lard. She will be down there all afternoon. The village elder can account for his family, but what he doesn't know is that the Moskali bastards are coming right over that hill, that hill right there.

The village elder knows his way of life is something to defend. It is a modest life, to have a bit of land and live from it. He tries to teach his babies Ukrainian, despite last year's laws or this year's occupiers. He doesn't know that when the Soviets arrive, they will flatten the hills, fill the ravines, hack the forest. They'll make the river foul, a smell like far-gone eggs. There will still be bugs, but meaner ones.

Or, perhaps, I am not giving him enough credit: perhaps he *does* have an inkling about the future, some vague trust in its formula. Oppression is a cyclic machine, and by this time he has already met many of its cogs—Knock, knock.

Who is that? The village elder isn't sure.

Knock, knock.

He doesn't know, though he has a hunch.

Knock, knock, knock.

Indeed, it was only a matter of time, the village elder thinks, the calendar on the wall blowing noisily as the door flings open, a rush of men that look like him.

Maybe one day we'll return to the village, though we certainly won't recognize—Tick, tick, readied guns—

We won't know where we are.

ON OUR WAY HOME FROM THE REVOLUTION

The house smells of onions, though Busia isn't using onions today. It is morning and my Ukrainian grandmother is frying eggs, but every pan is coated in grease from decades of wilting onions. Their sap is difficult to wash off. I spend my summers in her Chicago-area kitchen, admiring its retro brown and orange wallpaper. A sticky mirror hangs above the microwave. Wooden spoons showcase flavors from meals long ago. Beige onion papers blow across the counter whenever someone opens the back door. They collect like dead leaves between the stove and refrigerator, a ravine of lost leaves. We try not to look down there.

In village, you know we have our own chickens, she says over the popping oil. I nod. Busia has told me about her Ukrainian village and the old family farm many times.

Cow, pigs, chickens, big garden, potato, beets, cabbage . . . She flips the eggs with a melted, plastic spatula. *You know, Sonichka, we work all day. No television.* But she doesn't say *television* how I do. It is, instead, *tele-VEEZ-ion.* My Ukrainian grandmother mixes up her tenses in English, too. She doesn't fuss over the past and present, or the present and future, blending together.

Tele-VEEZ-ion. What she means is that I have it easy. I watch *Seinfeld* reruns and walk to the ice cream shop and read books. When she was a teenager, she worked the land.

Well, we have cow, until father leaves. Busia slides the greasy eggs onto a plate and sets them before me. She pours kettle water onto the pan. Onion water. She lowers her sciatica legs into a chair beside me, *Oi oi oi.*

Knock, knock, her arms shaking, the muscles loose and hanging. *They take father and that's it—gone.* She smacks her lips, *Nema, vse.* He's gone, that's all.

I hear allusions to this story a hundred times. As far as I can gather, my great-grandfather was a landowner and honorary mayor of his western Ukrainian village. Sometime after Stalin came to power, my great-grandfather resisted the collectivization orders. One day, strange men showed up at Busia's house and took her father away. She never saw him again. I can't remember exactly which details of this story she told me, which were whispered by other family members, and which ones were born of my own hungry mind. Sometimes I worry that I am not remembering a true memory, but remembering instead only the last instance in which I expressed what I thought to be a memory. A reflection of a reflection.

That's why you no answer—An airplane interrupts her.

Busia's house is just a few miles from O'Hare International Airport, which has been called the world's busiest. After her father was taken and while the war was flattening her village, Busia and her siblings fled or were forced toward Germany. They gathered in a refugee camp. From there, they emigrated to the US, one by one.

Now, low-flying planes over Chicago disrupt our conversations and *Seinfeld* reruns. Sometimes I stand in the driveway and stare at the shiny airplane bodies. I imagine who's inside, the people sitting cross-legged up there, the flight attendant and her heavy beverage cart. I imagine how during turbulence the beverage cart could soar through the air like a battering ram. How it could release a downpour of tiny vodka bottles.

The airplane body shines. Its passengers might be musicians, or politicians, or Oprah coming home from vacation. Maybe they are little unaccompanied minors like me, children of split families who spend the summers with their foreign grandmothers. When the airplane goes over, we pause, or shout, or turn up the volume.

That's why no answer door, okay Sonichka? She wags her finger, knuckles swollen, 'r's rolled, the 'o' in my name dragged long as if she is singing. *Never trust.*

Okay, Busia, I know. She tells me to never trust, over and over again. In her mind I am a perennial child, gleaning her wisdom always for the first time.

Tell me, you still remember "Shche Ne Vmerla"? She is asking about the Ukrainian national anthem, and I am grateful for the change of subject.

Of course, Busia. And we sing together there in the kitchen before breakfast. *Dushu y tilo my polozhym za nashu svobodu* . . . I know all the words to another country's national anthem, but I add black pepper to the eggs because my palate is American. I was raised on spicy food, on Tabasco, on those little packets of hot sauce from Taco Bell. *Why you do that?* Busia asks. She is suspicious of the alterations my cousins and I perform on her cooking.

Because I like it, I smile.

Okay, fine. However you like.

The summertime village dances. The handsome partisan fighters passing through town. The foreign anthem. The pigs. The chickens. The purges. I grow into these images. Though I do not share them with strangers, they are what I think of when strangers ask me where I come from.

Wow! Quite a last name you've got . . .
Where's that from?
Is it Polish? Russian?
How old were you when you learned to spell that?
How many letters?
How do you say that?
Say it again?
Again?

In these everyday interrogations, I do not tell strangers about the pigs or the purges, but I think of them. They are my personal explanation for the gaggle of characters I must squeeze onto insurance forms and dictate during classroom introductions. *Thirteen,* I say, *half the alphabet. And I won the spelling bee in first grade.* The name is like an abbreviation, a stand-in for Beets, and the river Ikva, and Lingonberry tea, and Onion grease, and the family Cow . . .

Busia's little images help me explain myself to myself, and so I grow into them. Or, perhaps it's more accurate to say I fall in love with them. I grow so fond of Busia's life in the old country that I want to make it my own. My surname spans like a line of hills, toothing the horizon. It has been assigned to me, but somehow it doesn't fit here. (*Where's that from?*) And when I add pepper to my plate, my grandmother grows suspicious, as if I don't belong to her kitchen either. But this name has been assigned to me, and I want to call it mine.

I.

It was the summer of 2013, and Ukraine was not in the American news. In Ukraine, the gardens were growing as usual, and *babushki* were bent over the leafy rows, and all was quiet on the Eastern Front. In summer 2013 Ukrainian news was like this:

UKRAINE INTERNATIONAL AIRLINES OPENS NEW
ROUTES.
POLITICIANS DISCUSS ABOLISHING DAYLIGHT SAV-
INGS TIME.
TAEKWON-DO SUMMER CAMP HELD IN CRIMEA.

The president, Viktor Yanukovych, was a crook and everyone
knew this, but it was a boring fact. Across Ukraine, the gardens
were growing and corruption was business as usual. It was, for
the most part, a safe place to live.

For me, the summer of 2013 was like this: An urgent sense
that I must see the last living relatives in Busia's village, our ancestral village. I was only 24 years old, but our relatives seemed
ancient. They could die soon, and the pigs with them. Although I had visited Ukraine and the village before, this was not
enough. I wanted the satisfaction of being called a local, and so
I accepted an English teaching position at a university in western Ukraine. I would leave at the end of summer with interme-
diate "kitchen" Ukrainian on the back of my tongue.

I began preparing visa documents while my boyfriend worried. We had met just a few months before I was due to leave the
country and decided that long distance would not be a problem
for *our* relationship. We met under what felt like fated circumstances: both of us were travelers in a town flanked by moun-
tains. It was fate that brought us together and so we were certain
fate would carry us through this period of separation. We were
surely not the first starry-eyed lovers to think so. He was an
organic farmer in Montana, and the idea of this charmed me.
Maybe farm life was to be my inheritance. Our babies would
play hide-and-seek in the corn stalks. We would feast from our
own yard. I was less charmed, however, when he began to nag.

What if you're over there and something happens? he said.

Like what? I asked.

What if Russia invades or something?

I could barely conceive of it. As far as I could tell, Putin and Yanukovych got along great. Ukraine may not be prosperous, but it was peaceful.

Putin has gone rogue and Ukraine is next door . . . Will you promise to come back if something happens? he begged.

I let out a laugh like a bark. I could admit this man was older and more experienced than me in certain areas, but he was not more experienced in post-Soviet affairs. By then I had already lived in Belarus and the Republic of Georgia. I spoke Ukrainian and some Russian. I read the *Economist* and subscribed to the *New York Times*. He was a farmer who had not been interested in Eastern Europe until meeting me. I smiled at his ignorance, but a small offense bloomed inside.

My family is from there. Do you think I'm stupid?

Of course not, he paused. *But anything can happen.*

No, I told him, not anything can happen. It was going to be a boring political year. There were no scheduled elections, no wildly controversial legislation—nothing like the previous year's language law that had stoked animosity between Russian and Ukrainian speakers. Sure, the president is corrupt, I explained, but the people voted him into power. And as for Putin, he is awful, and he is a meddler, but military invasion would be senseless. I could not imagine a situation that would cause him to do something so rash.

My boyfriend remained skeptical, which upset me further. I refused to make any promise about returning home, but finally muttered some platitudes about "staying safe," in order to end the discussion.

I cringe now when I think back to that conversation over six years ago. I wince at just how young I was then. I know he cringes too, but for different reasons. He later admitted that he thinks maybe vocalizing our fears breathes life into them, like mouth-to-mouth energy, the smallest breeze stirring a thing into being.

What, like you caused it? I ask.

I don't know, he says.

I don't know either, but I do know an important Russian superstition. I once saw a video interview of journalist Anna Politkovskaya, a famous critic of the Kremlin. She was fiercely opposed to the war in Chechnya and lived under constant state surveillance. In the video, the interviewer asks her about her deepest fear, and she refuses to answer. *You should never voice out loud what you are most afraid of,* she says, citing a Russian superstition. *If you talk about a disaster, you can cause it to happen.* Sometime after the interview, she was murdered in the elevator of her Moscow apartment building.

I don't know either, but it is strange how the match of one fruit seller in Tunisia lit the whole Arab Spring. I wonder what would have happened if the local authorities in Sidi Bouzid had just picked a different day to bother him. What if they hadn't confiscated his ripest melons, but only the sad-looking ones? What if a neighbor had smothered the fire on his coat? Or the fruit seller's wife had called on the telephone?

Now it's after the revolution, and I wonder about fate until I fall asleep. In these moments I am like a child again, holding bugs and marbles up to the light for a closer look. I am poking at my bellybutton, trying to feel where I came from.

II.

Before hopping a German airplane from New York to Vienna to Lviv, I am in Busia's kitchen discussing family history.

Do you know what it means—Bolsheviki? She often asks me this.

Yes, Busia, I know. The communists.

Tak, tak. Yes, yes. *Bad men.* Knock, knock and that's all. Never heard from again.

In this kitchen we use "Bolshevik" and "Communist" interchangeably because my grandmother was long gone by the time Stalin suggested replacing the first name with the second. At times "Russian" serves as a stand-in for both of these. But in discussing family history, the *Bolsheviki* are always nearby. And while it is not accurate to say that I came from the Bolsheviks, surely I would not be the same person if it weren't for them. Perhaps that knock on the door is and was and will always be knocking.

In the fall of 2013 I rode a German plane into Lviv, Ukraine. It was a beautiful season, the orange leaves in Stryiskyi Park filling up the gullies. They appeared soft beneath the curve of Austrian-looking street lamps. While I basked in Lviv's leftover European aesthetics, the news around me buzzed with talk of some other Europe.

After years of diplomatic discussions, the European Union and Ukraine were set to sign an Association Agreement, a monumental accord that would set Ukraine on a trajectory toward deeper integration with Europe. As part of the EU's Eastern Partnership agenda, the agreement would mark Ukraine's first move to eventual full membership. Leaders from the EU and Ukraine would meet in Vilnius, Lithuania, in November to close the deal.

In practical terms, the agreement would liberalize trade relations and visa regimes. Ukrainians could finally do their shopping in Poland visa free, for example. Theoretically, it would force President Viktor Yanukovych's administration to curb government corruption. Conservative estimates put his stolen wealth at $24 billion. Ideologically, it offered a choice, a turn toward certain values and away from others. For many this shift was equated with East and West—that is, from the "Russian"

East to the "European" West. Polls showed that at least 50% of the country supported the deal. Although more Russified Eastern Ukrainians were not, on the whole, excited at the prospect of closer ties with "decadent" Europe, analysts assumed that their tendency toward political apathy would facilitate the agreement regardless. And despite the challenges it could pose to his bumbling despotism and cozy relationship with the Kremlin, even Yanukovych had, on several occasions since taking office in 2010, indicated his serious intention to sign the agreement. It seemed inevitable the deal would be made.

I sat in Lviv's Austro-Hungarian-themed coffee shops, discussing Ukraine's EU aspirations with some friends. I was prone to a simple, homegrown analogy, Busia's pan oil cracking in the background. The move into the EU would be akin to sloughing off an abusive ex-lover (Russia), and turning instead to bat your lashes at the handsome, well-established fellow at the end of the bar (Europe! Human Rights! Enlightenment!). There was, I thought, nothing to lose. The agreement should be signed.

While the media talked of Vilnius, I was teaching English to journalism graduate students at Ukrainian Catholic University. Though Lviv is often considered the country's most Western-leaning and pro-European city, the university's strong reputation attracted scholars from all regions of Ukraine, East and West. My students were diverse, but they shared something: youth. Nearly all of them were post-Soviet babies. As the university's president would write later, "This is the generation of Ukrainians who were born and grew up in independent Ukraine, those uninfected by the virus of Soviet totalitarianism."

Recognizing the freshness of this sample cohort, I asked my students in early November to write about the upcoming Vilnius Summit where the Association Agreement was due to be signed. I figured they would support it. From our very first meeting, my students had greeted me as if we were old friends.

Ms. Bilocerkowycz. They said my name the same way I did, on the first try, no strange looks, no questions asked. My name was at home among them. It sounded like a song.

And so, when I asked them to write about the EU, I expected them to confirm what I already thought. The essays they submitted, however, were more layered and complicated. The students reflected on the obvious benefits of closer ties with Europe—it would help restrict the tyranny and kleptocracy of the ruling class—while also detailing potential pitfalls. Europe may be a good example for Ukrainian progress, but it was not a cure-all; it was not quick fix. And while many of the students approached Russia with caution, they were also closer to it. They had cousins and friends and childhood memories there, long train rides there, summers at the sanatorium, grandmothers in Smolensk. The word *self-determination* appeared in more than one essay. They were concerned about losing it to the EU, not—as I had assumed—to Russia. Perhaps this was because, for the better part of their history, they had been coping with Russia's stifling politics. They were, in a way, used to it. Though my students largely supported EU integration, they acknowledged that Europe was still an unknown devil.

Two weeks later on November 21, our class met in the late afternoon, the sun looking low and sad over our university's concrete suburb. I had planned a lesson on satire in the American context, and it was meant to amuse. We were scanning articles from *The Onion* as evidence.

U. S. ON VERGE OF FULL-SCALE GOVERNMENT HOE-
DOWN.
ASSAD UNABLE TO CONVINCE PUTIN THAT HE USED
CHEMICAL WEAPONS ON SYRIANS.
FDR, STALIN, CHURCHILL MEET FOR MUTTON LUN-
CHEON, NAP.

Although usually engaged and happy to banter across the room in brave bouts of English, my students turned sluggish. They were switching to Ukrainian and Russian, and they were whispering. They scrolled their news feeds under the desks, screen light glinting off their eyeballs, a reflection of a reflection of the country. I had brought in articles meant to make them laugh, yet somehow they were gloomier than before. I feared the worst but was nervous to ask. I let them out early.

The Ukrainian government was being strong-armed. Putin and Prime Minister Medvedev threatened sanctions. One journalist described it as a "tug of love" between Europe and Russia for Ukraine's affection. I don't disagree with this word choice. Love can be jealous and spiteful. It can be mean.

Seven days before the Vilnius Summit, Ukrainian cabinet ministers ordered the government to suspend any further action on the Association Agreement. *Nema, vse.* They suggested Ukraine ought to pursue a Kremlin-backed trade union with Belarus, Kazakhstan, and Russia instead. It was a matter of "national security."

For my students it was: a door slamming.

Later that night, a Kabul-born, Kyiv-based journalist, Mustafa Nayyem, appealed to his compatriots on Facebook. "Come on guys, let's be serious," he said. "If you really want to do something, don't just 'like' this post. Write that you are ready, and we can try to start something." By midnight there were 1,000 people gathered in the capital's central square, Maidan Nezalezhnosti, Independence Square.

Eight hours away in Lviv, inside the dormitory where I lived and where my students also lived, that night was a burst of flags, coats, gloves, markers, poster board. The building was all tile, no carpet. Apparently, it had been designed by an American architect, and we used to joke that you could hear someone drinking tea three floors above. Tonight, the hallways rang with specific plans. Students shouted to one another, giddy and agitated, about meeting in Lviv's central square. A group of approximately 30 people gathered there, mostly students, a few Americans, a Russian journalist. The students wrote in block letters a message back to their comrades in the capital. Кияни виходьте на Майдан. Kyivites go out on Maidan.

It is an awful cliché to say that a window opens, but it has that shape.

+++

Over the weekend in Kyiv some 40,000 people marched on Maidan in the numb, November air. The crowd was labeled young, liberal, academic. The week following was marked by free music, art installations, videos—what my Russian journalist friend Ivan called *hipster protests*—projected from the stone steps of the square. Everything was shared online as #Euromaidan or, simply, #Maidan. Buses arrived from all over the country, carrying protestors and their fat, down-feather coats.

Back in Lviv I am bundled in a yellow down jacket, observing the crowd of several thousand that had gathered on the city's own Maidan. I am camped high on a cement ledge with a few American friends. We are in awe. A man with a megaphone explains how they are organizing vans and carpools to Kyiv. Donations are being collected. A couple in their mid-20s, scarves spun up to their eyes, passes out blue-and-yellow ribbons with safety pins. I take one for my coat. We sing the national anthem *a capella* into the night sky, and I am a child again, at Ukrainian summer camp in the hills of Wisconsin, belting our ancestral song over the cicadas' compline. *Dushu y tilo my polozhym za nashu svobodu.* Soul and body we will lay down, for our freedom. I was born to be here, I think. It is fate. This, the greatest romance of my life. A miracle. Revolution, a real-life miracle! Revolution is a flaming bush.

I am charmed as I've never been before. I forget about sleep, and we spend the rest of the night playing the what-if game over beers, poking at all the corners of this new, glowing thing.

But by Friday the 29th, the closing day of the botched Vilnius Summit, the crowd in Kyiv has dwindled. It is clear no one in a position of power is actually listening to the protestors. Some students remain on the square, though talk has shifted from imminent demands to strategies for the next election. It is freezing outside, difficult conditions for a sustained demonstration. As I watch the quieting live streams from my dorm room in Lviv, it seems Maidan will remain just a blip on history's screen, an isolated spike in levels. I keep the heat in my room cranked high that winter. I turn the radiator up full blast and walk around in summertime shorts. It is selfish. I do not have to pay the gas bill. The university has also loaned me a set of screaming orange bed sheets. Their color bleeds into my clothes whenever I wash them. They are the color of heat.

I sit on my hot orange bed sheets in my too-hot room, watching the winter revolution. There are good guys and bad guys, and I am on the side of good. I was born to be here. Crack, crack, crack like fire. Like fate. My computer battery burns the tops of my thighs. My legs leave sweat marks on the sheets. Hot. Heat. Wet sheets. I play footsie with the cord, with the whole country. Knock, knock. I have arrived. This is how my grandmother's land will become mine. This is how I will earn my name. The crowds are dwindling, but I pray it isn't over yet. Revolutions require heroes, and I wish to be one.

On Saturday morning, the country wakes to videos of Kyiv riot police descending on the Maidan at 4:00am with bulky black tactical gear, billy clubs, tear gas, stun grenades. The riot police are called *Berkut,* which means golden eagles, and they descend just like that. They beat and kick the few protestors left sleeping on the square. In one video clip, a photographer wearing a Reuters press coat snaps pictures while blood freezes on his forehead. In others, young men are curled into fetal balls on the pavement, blocking the blow of boots from their faces. The violence looks random, haphazard, indiscriminant, though its cover of darkness is certainly intentional.

Years from now, in some future, I will see an image that reminds me of the Berkut's 4:00 am raid. I will be camping on the Olympic peninsula when I see it. Our campsite is lush and secluded, a curtain of ferns on every side. The acoustics are such that you can hear a whisper from the opposite end of the grove. When we pack up to leave, no sooner do we shut the car door than a swarm of crows descends on our spot. They pick through the fire pit. They catwalk across the picnic table, making eye contact with us the entire time. From inside our car, we watch the oily birds take what crumbs they want, squawking and gloating in our ears.

A Ukrainian government spokesman explains that the square needed to be cleared in order to make room for the city's annual Christmas tree. Aren't you tired of sleeping in the cold? he suggests. It's time for Christmas. A skeleton of the usual tree is put up, but officials do not get any further in decor. The tree structure rises above Maidan like the bones of a bonfire, like the towering *vatra* we used to have on the last night of summer camp. Yanukovych may have hoped to extinguish the final little remnants of protest, but his plan backfires. The country is a live wire. It is livid.

Around this time I learn about a woman that my boyfriend has been with. He and I were not technically together when it happened, and the fact of it not being a formal transgression feels, somehow, worse. That is, I have no right to be angry about it. The other woman is an artist, a bohemian lady with an unusual name and prominent eyebrows. I learn of their liaison and something inside my chest starts to scald. I click through her page, photo after photo.

Her in Berlin.

Her perfect eyebrows.

Her with a canvas. (She is more interesting than I am.)

Her with an artistic filter.

Her with a wine glass.

Her with a hat. (She can wear hats in a way I cannot.)

Her in a museum.

Her eyes, extra green. (Greener than mine.)

Her eyebrows, brooding.

I click my way into a small, jealous fury. I want her dead. I want to be her. But I am also happy to have something to lob at my boyfriend, a gas canister to set off inside our bedroom when he least expects it.

As I click uneasily through video after video of the Berkut beating protestors, my chest feels scorched. I am furious at the regime. I am jealous of the protestors. I am also, oddly, pleased. Now this, *this* is ammunition. Violence can be leveraged, I think. We can work with this.

As I click, it becomes apparent that I will get to claim Ukraine in a way that my family living in Chicago or even in the village cannot. My relatives in rural Ukraine do not have indoor plumbing, much less a television or computer. They are aging, and the pigs alongside them. They will receive the news days later by twisted word-of-mouth, or radio snippets. They will not watch the revolution go viral as I do. Somehow, this Ukraine is becoming mine, though, with my blue American passport, I will not be the one paying for it.

Is that what it means to *be mine?* To love something into a jealous fury? The battery sits hot on my lap. I let it burn.

III.

The day after the Berkut crackdown, Kyiv explodes. Conservative estimates say 300,000 people flooded the city center on Sunday, while other sources claim as many as 800,000. By night the standoff between protestors and police turns violent. Riots erupt.

Are you being safe? my boyfriend asks a thousand different times over Skype that winter. He sends links to articles, snippets of dark news to justify his queries. *You promised.*

I'm trying, I reply, hoping it is true. I watch him through the computer screen, but he is like an imaginary person there, a set of pixels, a faraway plane. I do not mention that I have taken to Facebook-stalking his old bohemian lover.

Classes at the university are cancelled for nearly a month. The administration recognizes that agency and fate don't often line up so neatly. They encourage students to add their bodies to the crowd in Kyiv, to organize local demonstrations, to publish articles and appeals. The faculty sit in awe of their students, acknowledging them as a national resource. "They are now leading their generation's very own mega-scale 'workshop' on human dignity and solidarity in Ukraine," the university president writes on the school website in December.

I, too, am in awe of the students, but see how drained they are, coming and going from meetings on campus. I explain the situation to my boyfriend, who is still far away, somewhere in America: *My head is running 1,000 miles a minute. There is so much crazy energy here. I see it in my students' eyes. They are not well. My colleagues are tearing up around the water cooler. The administration is facing intimidation tactics from the authorities.*

The woman who is the chair of our department, Halyna, cries to me over coffee in the office one afternoon. *This is the third revolution of my lifetime,* she says, leaning heavily against the cabinet. *I'm so tired.*

After the Berkut violence in Kyiv, it became, what my students called, a "different Maidan," which means this: the young, liberal opposition was joined by an older, more conservative crowd of Ukrainians. War medals, blue collars, men with grizzled chins. They brought very useful supplies, too. Canvas army tents, thick steel spikes, rope, barrels, wooden swords, gas masks, pallets, barbed wire, heaps of lumber and axes, cook stoves, shields, green helmets left over from another war. Together the protestors, old and young, claimed a half-mile stretch of the road around Maidan, including the Kyiv City Council building, whose new purpose was tagged with spray paint on the front: Штаб Революції. Revolution Headquarters. The occupied building became a makeshift clinic, press center, cafeteria, art gallery, and shelter for the sleepy. Outside the occupied government building, an elaborate tent city was established. Activists provided free services for each other. There were soup tents, tea tents, a prayer tent, and a tech tent where phones and laptops could be charged. One local journalist said downtown Kyiv was now a "starry-eyed commune."

It was like a modern fairy tale, a Middle Ages town made of crude and unusual 20th-century trash. Around the occupied territory, protestors constructed immense barricades to deter police incursion. The structures were made of sandbags, old wooden furniture, hundreds and hundreds of car tires, dumpster lids, bricks, shipping crates, gnarled shapes of metal and tin, origins unknown. Protestors piled whatever they could find. They topped the walls with barbed wire and flags, and calcified everything in ice, as the temperature that winter rarely got above freezing. In the small hours of one December night, police tried again to clear the square, but Maidan was ready for the surprise swarm of black jackets. The barricades held.

In Lviv, I try to keep my head down. I watch the 24-hour live streams from my dorm room, volume muted, radiator blazing through my nightmares. I am not making plans to go to Kyiv. I am not writing articles. I am even careful about how I word outgoing emails. The university administration is not shy about its opposition to the regime, and thus we are all suspects. Years later, it is easy to forget one key fact: during the revolution, nobody knows if the revolution will succeed.

So I keep quiet and wait for my boyfriend to come visit. He purchased a flight in early November, long before Vilnius, and despite the grim news reports, I know he isn't going to give up the ticket. Though he seems concerned, I hear something else in his Skype-skewed voice. Jealousy, perhaps, a fear of missing out, a tinge of envy. In our sentences, love and revolution become muddled. At first, *I feel strongly about the good of the [Ukrainian] nation because you do. I care about the fate of the people because you did first.* And later, *Why are we arguing over dates, while the martyrs are dying for their 'free Ukraine'?* And later still, *I could live in this new Ukraine with you.* Revolution is the most romantic thing we can imagine.

When my boyfriend arrives in mid January, the daily highs hover around 15°F. We bundle in long coats, and wool socks, and scarves up to our shining eyes to walk the cobblestone streets of Lviv's old town. We order *borshch* and sausages and mulled wine. We read the news from Kyiv aloud each morning, politics over instant coffee. We climb Vysoky Zamok, the highest point in town, where we can see ruins of the old castle through the trees. I try not to think about the bohemian woman. I do not want my jealousy to spoil our nice time. I do not mention her name, though she is always nearby.

How do you say 'I love you'? he asks.

Ya tebe lyublyu.

There are Old World pigeons outside our window. There is snow shrouding the statue of the poet. There are red, yellow, orange headscarves on the crowns of *babushki* at the market. Revolution drones in the background. The anthem is sung on the hour, every hour, *a cappella* from the square.

If not for these, would it have been love? Do we fall in love with people, or do we love ourselves in a place and time?

On Friday, January 17, President Yanukovych signs a set of laws that were rammed through parliament the day before. The legislation criminalizes "extremist activity" and includes, among other points, an anti-mask law, provisions for internet censorship, amnesty for officers accused of committing crimes against protestors, heavy penalties for "defamation" or disseminating information about Berkut officers, and jail time for unauthorized installation of tents, stages, or sound equipment. *The Economist* notes the measures were "inspired by Moscow's laws." Maidan activists call them simply "dictatorship laws."

In the evening, we are sharing a piece of chocolate cake at a Viennese-style café in the city center. I am writing. My boyfriend is reading a book of philosophy, a title I can't recall. My phone buzzes with an SMS from Ivan. *You guys should come to Kiev for weekend. Demonstrations will be huge because of Yanukovych and despot laws. Should be fun.*

A Muscovite, Ivan has been reporting from Maidan since the movement started. Despite his usual air of flippancy (*hipster protests*), he is sympathetic to the Ukrainian cause and writes thoughtful articles for Lenta.ru, a heavily trafficked online newspaper. *Lenta* is widely considered one of the last high quality independent news sources in Russia.

Vanya wants us to go to Kyiv, I tell my boyfriend.

He smiles with his eyes. I like being able to tell what he wants by the angle of his laugh lines. *Well, let's go then.*

Really? I say.

Why not?

I don't know, I say, though I do. He has no responsibilities to Ukraine—no family, no work, no history. His name is Irish, which means he has not been interrogated as I have. He is free to move about, rootless and haphazard. He gets to be spontaneous, while I must be careful. I am hard at work staking a claim to this land, doing my best to avoid upsetting the violent regime. I am reminded of his recklessness and am irritated he ever had the nerve to worry about me.

Actually, you know, there's a reason I haven't gone to Maidan yet. I really was trying to be safe, like we talked about.

I know, he says. *But Vanya is practically a local. It will be fine if we are all there together.*

I consider this for a moment. He is right, Vanya would make a suitable guide. And I wonder what a trip to the revolution would make me—a tourist, or a real Ukrainian, or someone else entirely. I imagine my surname, stretched wide as the southern steppe. And the Cossacks are on their way, the Berkut are on their way, the Berkut are riding, black birds coming right over that hill, that barricade right *there.*

We take an overnight train to the capital. I do not sleep well on the hard bunk. In the gunmetal morning, Kyiv's main station looks disinterested. It doesn't care if we are there. I am knocking at the city's front door, but no one cares. We are a boring fact.

Our breath rises high above the frigid platform, as if we have smoking garbage bins in all four lungs. Barrels burning to keep us warm.

IV.

Before the revolution, whenever someone spoke of *revolution,* I pictured a barricade. It was an old barricade, like an oil-painted version of 19th-century France. And when I pictured a barricade in the French rue, I saw that dove-cheeked child from *Les Miserables.* And when I saw her face I heard a song or a command, desperate and hopeful, *To the barricades!* I heard this in my own language, not in the language it would have originally been. *Barricade* is from the French *barrique,* which means *barrel,* as in: oak cask, as in: the wedding miracle, as in: drink of lovers.

It is after the revolution now, and so the barricade is slowly becoming French again. But that January morning, when I floated up from the Metro station into the 7:00am heart of Kyiv and saw myself surrounded by 20-foot barricades, I admit, I did not think of France at all. I thought of America.

I tried to imagine these same junk piles in Washington, DC, but I had no idea where we would find so many tires. Would Home Depot donate sand bags? Sheet metal? Or is the CEO of Home Depot golf buddies with the current administration? How far outside the city must one drive to buy barbed wire? Because, it seemed, we would need miles of it.

A priest chants morning prayers from the stage. Wood-burning stove smoke swells like incense over the barricades. Stubbly war veterans emerge from their tents holding Styrofoam teacups. They mumble about the day's events, the dictatorship laws. The government's one-time Christmas tree looms. It is now covered in Ukrainian flags and opposition symbols, no longer green, but rainbow. Below our feet, underneath the barricades of Maidan, there is a modern mall stocked with international brands. Down there, people are shopping.

My boyfriend and I meet up with Ivan and wander through Maidan. We take photos of ourselves, collect free stickers, sip coffee, and browse names written on a wall of bricks. It is the guestbook of the revolution, and most of the names remind me of my own, those tumbling clusters of consonants, those *-vychs* and *-wyczs* and *-enkos* and *-chuks.* It is like a holiday craft fair from some medieval dream. I still do not know who I am to this revolution, so I do not write my name on a brick.

The temperature this morning is mean. We cannot last long outside, and eventually the three of us take shelter in a nearby café. Kupidon, which means *cupid,* is tucked in a basement. A LVIV-STYLE ART CAFÉ—THE LAST REFUGE FOR UKRAINIAN INTELLECTUALS! We drink beer and order *borshch.* Ivan keeps his laptop close, reading us news blurbs and status updates, as if taking the pulse of Maidan. At neighboring tables people warm their hands over soup and swipe their phones. It is a normal café day, except the customers are wearing balaclavas. The waiters seem not to notice. Revolution plays on the bar TV.

The Sunday crowd is large and angry. Protestors march toward parliament via Hrushevskoho Street, but are met by a police cordon and a blockade of military vehicles. Riot police warn the protestors over loudspeakers that, under new legislation, their actions are illegal. The crowd responds with rage at the very notion, their rage paired with pipes, helmets, and poor man's grenades. It is late afternoon.

We should go, Ivan says over his computer, face blue from the glow. *It's finally happening.*

Why finally? I ask. *Why do you want violence?* The question is probably more meant for myself.

It's the only way they will listen. He gestures with his cigarette to a few other journalists we'd met in the café. *Let's go have a look!* It is casual, as if we are going to have a look at a pond full of minnows, or at the home furnishings section of a department store.

My boyfriend and I exchange quick glances across the table. I assume we are both moderating the same debate. I cannot articulate why I would go watch a violent revolt, but neither can I say a good reason not to go. If we are worried about safety, then we have already been too close to the clashes all day.

So that's a yes then? Ivan asks.

There is a prick in my chest. An old pang of greed. I want to be the bohemian woman. I want her brooding eyebrows. I want her dead. The basement café is very warm today, so many bodies in here, lots of wool and down-feather coats. Revolution drones in the background. I want to be her. I want to hurl her profile pictures across the table, a torrent of lunchtime bullets, and I want to control exactly how each one hits. The inner thigh. The breastplate. I want this man across the table to take me seriously. It's the only way they will listen.

Okay, I say. *Let's go.*

And the words are barely out of my mouth before there is a smear of rainbow-stained bills on the table, and we are running down, down, down the hill to Maidan.

+++

A man with a cross on his coat hands us facemasks while we are at full sprint. Past the tent city. Past the stage. Someone with a microphone is trying to calm the protestors. Past the barricades. Black cloud rolls across the frontline of the clashes, only 200 meters from us now. Stun grenades make a loud, seamless thunder. There is a stream of young men running toward the police. They wear gasmasks and helmets. They carry sticks and plywood shields with spray-painted *tryzubs,* the Ukrainian coat of arms. Some carry cobblestones they just pulled up from the road. Others haul boxes of glass bottles and rags for Molotov cocktails. We reach for each other, my boyfriend and I, and there is an unspoken agreement to hang back while Ivan runs ahead. A car whips through the crowd right beside us. It is a black Audi, and a man in a tailored business suit hurries out of it. He unloads several crates of bottles and a few tires for burning. He whips away again.

We cough from the tear gas. My chest stings, and I cannot catch a breath. My boyfriend will say later that it was like an asthma attack, only external, the size of a whole city. Like the whole city is having an attack. The air taut and dangerous. He is a child again, gulping for oxygen, for whatever God will listen.

I do not have asthma. I am not familiar with its tug and pull the way he is, so instead it is: a friend, living in New York, renting a basement room in Crown Heights. She doesn't notice the build-up because it's mostly odorless. But her upstairs neighbor notices and warns her that something is wrong—something is really, really wrong inside their home. There has been gas leaking for days. The building is a balloon full of bad air. Cubic foot upon cubic foot of flammable air. A house waiting to kill you. Air so taut it could kill you.

Can you imagine? my friend is still frantic when she speaks of it. *What if I had lit a candle, just one?*

And then it happens. Swipe of stick, the clang of an incense burner. Something scares the jittery crowd and in a swift moment people are sprinting back toward us. *Get back!* I see something I never have before—a face in flight. *Get back!* I have never seen anyone flee, I think. Flight is wide-eyed. It is screaming at strange men, eyes wide. It is leaving your village on foot as fast as you can, abandoning the cow. *Get back!* Flight is leaving behind the pigs because if the Soviets don't get you, the Nazis will. Flight is boarding a plane to an unknown continent, asking for *borshch* after landing in New York and being laughed at. It is your face, blank as an egg. A fleeing woman touches my arm.

Women get back! she screams at me in Ukrainian. *Women to the barricades!*

I want to tell her to just ignore me, that I don't belong here anyway. I reach for my boyfriend's hand, and we move out of the way. *Women to the barricades!* They run by us. We hang back near the doorway of a posh hotel, the Hotel Dnipro, the first place I ever stayed in Ukraine when I came to visit with my family in 2007. I push the image of my father from my mind. I don't want to think about what he would say now. He has been emailing for weeks, begging me to be careful, to please consider crossing the border into Poland, to please keep an extra bag packed, just in case.

We continue to watch the chaos from the Dnipro doorway. Men and boys running toward the police; women running away. I think about the piglets on my boyfriend's farm back in Montana, though Montana itself feels like an imaginary place, a faraway airplane carrying made-up people. They were so skittish, those Montana piglets. They would scare themselves into scuttling around the trough in a swarm. I could sit and watch them for hours, laughing at their circle dance, round and around the feeder. At the end of the season, we would swoop down and eat them. We would fry them for breakfast. But they didn't know that then. Back then, the only thing they had to be afraid of was themselves.

A carefully placed Molotov cocktail makes contact with an empty city bus and sets it ablaze. The thing burns black, black smoke, its black tendrils curling over the nervous crowd. It is like a perverted scene from *Animal Farm*, a drift of people moving in loops around the bus, Mr. Jones off drunk somewhere in the presidential palace, doing his best to forget the revolution. I don't know who I am in this metaphor. Everything is turning in on itself. It is a violent day on the family farm. The bus burns angry black, and all stories are then, now, soon-to-be. My throat prickles.

A pair of girls walks by. They are arm-in-arm, strolling. They are in the wrong painting. This is still Paris, but it is not the bloodied French rue. It is Sunday on La Grande Jatte. A woman with a parasol. A puppy off-leash. A gentle sailboat. The two girls are wearing high heels and extra short skirts. Their shoes are pointy like daggers, which is what stiletto means in Italian. They are giggling. Hair long and shiny, to the middle of their backs. They are dressed to the nines and must be on their way to a nightclub. *Typical Kyiv girls, oligarch daughters,* my expat friends and I would have joked. They don't seem to notice the revolution happening around them. They ignore the Molotov cocktails, and the black smoke, and the fleeing women. *Women to the barricades!* They must be gossiping, I think. They must be very self-absorbed. Why do they not care about the revolution? Later I will reconsider my judgment of them. Maybe, they know something we don't.

What is this? My boyfriend asks, staring at the pair. *A riot, or a girls' night out?*

I cough at him. It is the only response I can offer. The tear gas burns. I hiccup, tripping over some scorched scrap of word, some ancient name left in my throat. Besides, I don't have an answer anyways. I don't know why the oligarch daughters are so placid, or who I am in relation to them, or why we are here in the first place. There is only my lungs, raging. Just black cloud, waving.

We watch from the doorway for minutes, or hours. Eventually, my boyfriend suggests we leave because we are not doing anything. No one cares if we are here. We can't throw grenades at someone else's revolution. And we can't be tourists at a riot, he reasons. I don't want to admit he is right, though he probably is. I came wanting to collect ammo for myself. Something to hurl at the crooked president, something to aim at the man I was trying to love. Something to make him listen. *Do you think I'm stupid? My family is from here.* I wanted the revolution to love me back, but all I got were these silly images. Just black cloud, waving. The noise of gloating in my ear.

+++

Explosion sounds rattle the hostel windows all night long. We hold vigil in the common room, and young men slip in the front door one at a time. They remove their gasmasks and prop their wooden shields up against the shoe rack before nodding goodnight. Their faces are ashy as they fall into bunk beds. My boyfriend checks the day's NFL scores on the computer, and I cannot believe that someone, somewhere, is playing football.

The bombing noises continue in the morning light, and when I wake up, I'm not sure where I am or what century it is. I am watching my real life like it has just reached cruising altitude. It is a distant mirage. I think this means it is time to return home to Lviv. We say goodbye to Ivan and depart for the train station.

On our way, we stop at the Kyiv City Council Building, the so-called Revolution Headquarters, looking for a cup of coffee. Two hulking revolutionaries ask to see our passports at the door. They wear black balaclavas, only their eyes flickering through. One guard rubs his finger along the embossed eagle. It seems to be a rub of approval. *Welcome to Ukraine,* he says to me. I can tell he is grinning from his eyes, as he opens the door for us. I'm not sure who put this balaclava man in charge of welcoming us to Ukraine. What are his credentials? Does the country belong to him now? We move through the occupied building, stepping delicately over the limbs and ponytails of sleeping protestors. Or does it still belong to Busia? To our cousins in the village? To the oligarch daughters, or the fleeing women? I see that someone from Ukraine's far-right party has strung a portrait of nationalist figure Stepan Bandera from a balcony inside the hall. Does the country now belong to them? Or to the students in Lviv, who reportedly turned off the microphone when an ultra-nationalist MP took the Maidan stage? Does Ukraine belong to every starry-eyed couple asleep on the floor here?

At the train station, we settle into a four-bed coupé back to Lviv. There are two other passengers in our car, a Russian-speaking *babushka* and a younger Ukrainian-speaking woman, both solo travellers. The elderly woman opens a bag of hard-boiled eggs and proceeds to salt and eat them in large bites. Her eggs make our cabin stink. I gawk at her, blank-faced. I do not care about etiquette or the fact that I am staring. Her ritual is the most complicated thing I want to think about.

But the younger woman is eager to make conversation because she's never met an American before. She asks if young people in America are as addicted to their cell phones as her two kids are. I ask her about the Ukrainian word for *unicorn*. When I tell her that we just came from Maidan, she shakes her head at the sad situation there. She is worried for all the children.

In the middle of the night and before our arrival in Lviv, both women disembark at small town stations. We say our goodbyes in Russian and Ukrainian. I lock the cabin door behind them and turn to face my boyfriend. I can still hear explosions, a phantom echo from the long night. My head is pounding. *Get back!* Black smoke. The wide eyes of flight are everywhere, though we are alone now. *Women to the barricades!* Black cloud. The cabin is full of scorched air. We argue for a while, I'm not sure about what. I still do not say the bohemian woman's name, though I want so desperately to toss it at him, a flaming Molotov. I am angry, and I have no right to be. My head throbs, and I have no right to complain about that either. The revolution does not belong to me. I climb up to my boyfriend's bunk and huddle close on the starchy sheets, the train around us left over from an old empire. I say his name. My voice singes like a branding iron.

On our way home from the revolution, I just want something to call mine.

V.

While I was in Ukraine, Busia sat on a folding chair beside a dusty radio in her Chicagoland bedroom. In her town, you can hear a Ukrainian-language news program floating from the AM dial. During the revolution months, Busia listened to the litany of losses coming from Kyiv. She worried about me, I'm sure, *Oi Bozhe,* Oh God, crossing herself thrice for my safety, waiting on my name.

TWO DEAD IN UKRAINE FOLLOWING ANTI-GOVERN-MENT PROTESTS. The day after we returned to Lviv, the first two people were killed on Maidan. They were activists who received stray bullets to the heart during clashes on Hrushevskoho. Berkut were supposed to be using rubber bullets, but these ones were lead. The barrels had been switched. The first two dead were an ethnic Armenian and a Belarusian. The symbolism of their backgrounds—of a regional brotherhood fighting against post-Soviet oppression—seemed obvious to everyone.

UKRAINE'S BLOODIEST DAY. One month later a hundred people, both protestors and police, died in Kyiv when special forces opened sniper fire on the square. The oldest victim was in his 80s and the youngest was still in high school. One of the bodies belonged to my colleague at the university, a history lecturer who left behind his fiancée.

YANUKOVYCH FLED UKRAINE WITH ONLY HAND LUGGAGE. After the bloodshed on Maidan, Yanukovych lost his job. He fled by helicopter in the middle of the night to somewhere in Russia. Activists descended on his stolen palace at Mezhyhirya and fished documents out of the Dnipro River that verified the sums of his corruption and regimented brutality. A few of my students helped in the drying and preservation effort, which took place in the ex-president's boathouse and wooden sauna.

The name Paul Manafort also emerged from the river. The American political advisor had been a consultant to Yanukovych and his Party of Regions for nearly a decade. Manafort helped Yanukovych get elected in 2010, despite the fact that

Yanukovych's team had been accused of massive voter fraud in the 2004 election when he ran against Viktor Yushchenko. And so, after the revolution, Yanukovych fled and Manafort lost his biggest paying job, too.

PUTIN MOVES AGAINST THE PRESS. In March Ivan lost *Lenta*. After it published an interview with an ultranationalist from Ukraine, the Kremlin cited the publication for extremism and forced its chief editor to resign. She was replaced by a progovernment editor. Ivan and nearly all of his colleagues quit the journal in protest, accusing the government of censorship.

UKRAINE CRIES 'ROBBERY' AS RUSSIA ANNEXES CRIMEA. In the weeks to follow, Ukraine lost whole swaths of its soil. Threatened by the stoutness of civil society and the failure of his man next door, Vladimir Putin punished his neighbor by annexing Crimea and invading the eastern region of Donbass. Putin claimed he was protecting Russian speakers from the "unconstitutional coup" that had taken place in Kyiv. The Russian Federation funneled supplies, ammunition, and troops into eastern Ukraine, taking control of several large cities. Reports indicate that the newly elected Ukrainian government responded with cluster bombs. What developed was a proxy war, involving Ukrainian government forces, Russian government forces, and Russian-backed separatists.

THE WAR NO ONE NOTICES IN UKRAINE. Since the fighting in Donbass began, over 10,000 people have lost their lives. Troops and civilians, Ukrainians and Russians, schoolteachers, and coal miners, and grandmothers. Another 1.5 million Ukrainian citizens have been internally displaced. Many are still roaming, fighting with bureaucrats for assistance. They wander between hostels, university dormitories, and Soviet-era sanatoriums, searching for a bedroom of their own.

+++

I returned to America on the eve of its Independence Day, 2014. Before leaving Ukraine, I left my yellow down overcoat with a friend. I didn't think I would be needing it again.

When I landed at JFK, the English-speaking passport control officers sounded like foreigners. They asked me questions about my last name, how long and difficult it must have been to learn. When they tried to pronounce it, I told them they did so perfectly, though of course I was lying. Later, I watched fireworks from a rooftop in Brooklyn while wearing a plastic *vinok*, a Ukrainian flower crown I brought from Lviv. The air up there was cool and loose, the brownstones clement, the whole neighborhood waving, *Welcome to this country.*

It happened one other time that summer, the air at ease and merciful. I was in Montana during high season on my boyfriend's farm. We had not seen each other since the winter. Together we climbed a mountain near the Canadian border and I felt it again. Wildflowers at ease. Moose and breeze and bear at ease. Up here, there were no purges, no militants. No tear gas blistering our throats. We were a million miles from anyone's crooked president, from the memorials and vendors of revolutionary kitsch that had since established themselves on the Maidan. Up here, animals drank glacier water without thought of mutiny. Here, we brushed shoulders with white, waving clouds. Soon after the mountain, my boyfriend asked me to marry him.

"These revolutions are born of hope," Crane Brinton wrote in his 1938 treatise, *The Anatomy of Revolution.* I had spent the last year riding a billow of hope. My students and colleagues and the young men in the hostel bunks beside me were all running on hope. Our department chair, Halyna, had seen revolution after revolution, had seen the way Ukraine's leaders, lifted up by the people, did and were and would always betray them. Despite the evidence, she still had faith that maybe this time would be different. When her teenage daughter asked to go to the revolution, Halyna crossed herself thrice and said, *Yes.*

His laugh lines were so pronounced when he asked me that question, and with hope lifting like a holy smoke in my lungs, I said it, too.

+++

After the revolution melted into a war, it became clear that the Ukrainian side needed help. The army was underfunded and ill-equipped. The Ukrainians were desperate for supplies, while the Russian state quietly funneled them across the border to its proxy fighters in Ukraine. After the revolution melted into a war, a collection was taken up at Ukrainian Catholic University where I continued to teach until July. All faculty and staff members agreed to donate part of their monthly salaries to the Ukrainian army. But I only heard about the collection after it was done. No one asked or expected me to make an offering. I was a tourist. I left the revolution with a headache, and that's all. My name is not mentioned in the litany Busia hears on AM radio. I did not have to pay.

MALAYSIA AIRLINES MH17 FLIGHT CRASH: 20 FAMI-LIES GONE IN ONE SHOT. While we were up on a mountain in Montana, kissing the cool air, an airplane was falling from the sky in Eastern Ukraine. Rebel fighters in the Donbass shot down Malaysia Airlines Flight 17 with a Russian-made Buk missile. The plane fell into a sunflower field. It had been bound for Kuala Lumpur from Amsterdam. It carried actresses, authors, senators, AIDS researchers, children, and grandfathers. Their body parts rained onto village roads and family gardens, went crashing through thatched roofs. Do you know how it feels to find a child's leg among the potatoes? An ear in the onions? I do not know. I was a tourist at a revolution. Do you know how it feels to abandon the cow and flee for your life? As we drove away from the mountain, the NPR radio correspondent spoke flatly about the crashing limbs, the fallen airplane.

After President Yanukovych fled in his helicopter and the dust settled on Maidan, Petro Poroshenko, another of Ukraine's oligarchs, was elected president. Almost five years later, he has failed to implement some of the most necessary anti-corruption reforms. For much of his term, Poroshenko's approval rating has hovered in the single digits. Despite Halyna's hope, the leaders eventually and always betray. They prove themselves to be the revolution's best opportunists, past, present, future, forever. With war raging on the Eastern Front, Kyiv is no longer a starry-eyed commune, until the next time it is.

My boyfriend and I fought for two years and then broke up. We did not get married, did not live up to the promises made. As much as I tried, I could not possess him. Maybe, I thought, if we shared a name, he could be mine. But such possession is not possible, for at any given moment there is an airplane falling from the sky. At any given moment there is a crooked president and a man with a ground-to-air missile and an innocent plane nearby. I have stopped thinking possession is possible because our very lives do not belong to us. Our names are not really ours.

We fought for two years. A million little offenses bloomed inside me, a million jealous doors slamming, and then we broke up. *Nema, vse.* He's gone, and that's all. This loss is not worth mentioning in any litany, and it is wrong for me to bring it up here. I was a tourist at a revolution. When strangers ask about my surname, I could tell them about barricades—about *barrique,* a barrel for wine, and a barrel for bullets, and how the first miracle was at a wedding, but later there was torture and nails and the body slouching dead. I could write a hundred stupid lines like that, all cheap and unearned.

Do we love people, or do we love ourselves in a place and time? Do I love my grandmother, or her onion-laced eggs, my face in the kitchen mirror? I brought home a souvenir from the revolution and gave it to Busia: a blue and yellow flag, the colors of Ukraine, beneath the European Union symbol, a circle of golden stars. She stuck the flag in a napkin holder, where it waves every time she opens the back door. We sit at the table. A window overlooks the rows of her long-ago garden. Her sciatica is too painful now for bending over the dirt. It is only weeds left. She keeps her dentures in a yogurt container and puts them in when it's time to eat. I pepper the food she serves me. We swap songs from the old country—an airplane rattles the teakettle.

They are love songs, mostly.

BLOODLINES
(OR, ALTHOUGH A GOOD MAN, A MUSCOVITE)

Sonechko, my grandmother breathes into her telephone. She is tethered to the kitchen wall by a cord. *Ah, sonechko prishla na vikonechku!* A ladybug came to my window. This pet name "sonechko" sounds like the Ukrainian word for sunshine, and the word for ladybug, and also like the diminutive of my name. This is how she greets me when I call. *Sonechko, how are you, my love?*

After our usual greeting, she likes to teach me things: Do not go outside with wet hair because you will catch a cold. Do not eat fish and milk in the same meal because you will get nausea. Do not sit on the ground or on a cold bench because your ovary eggs will freeze. Do not answer the door for a stranger because you will get stuffed into the trunk of a car and taken to the forest. *Sonechko*—she says, dead serious—*never trust.*

When I return from Ukraine at 25, I quickly move to Ohio for graduate school. Though I am sorry to have left Lviv, I am glad to be able to talk to Busia several times a week with ease. She does not have a cellphone or a computer, but she does have an ancient beige landline attached to the far wall of her kitchen. She cannot move around the house with it, and so she sits on an old box, twisting the cord around her ankle and telling me that I need to eat more.

Her name is Nina, but my cousins and I call her Busia (from *babusya*, Ukrainian for grandmother), and she is the mother of my father. Perhaps grandparents are prone to worry, but I've always noticed that my father's mother was more worried about things than my mother's mother. My mother's mother—whose parents were from Germany but who was herself born in America—might worry that rain was going to ruin the picnic. Busia, on the other hand, carries with her an existential dread, as if there's no need to worry about the picnic because we will surely be involved in a car accident on our way there. Her cynicism in these matters feels foreign, almost un-American, or at least a departure from our national tendency toward brutish optimism. Indeed, my Ukrainian grandmother is a pessimist. For a long time, I assumed this was because of the television.

You watch too much news, Busia, I tell her after she warns me for the hundredth time not to open the door for plumbers or electricians—even if something is broken—because servicemen have a nasty habit of being strangers. There are three TVs in my grandmother's house, though she is the only one living there now. The sets are usually tuned to WGN News Chicago, and for most of my life, I blamed those anchors and their nightly if-it-bleeds-it-leads broadcasting for my grandmother's unease.

It wasn't until I was old (maybe 20 or 21, which is to say, embarrassingly old) that I began to understand Busia's fear as something more primeval. It had less to do with WGN and more to do with her childhood in western Ukraine. She was, from what I can gather, a teenage village heartthrob. Handsome partisan fighters passing through town would stop to flirt with her and her two sisters. When I turned 18, Busia gave me a silver ring with *Dubno 1941* etched inside the band. It was a gift from a soldier. When I asked what his name was, she told me, *I not remember.*

Busia quit attending school around sixth grade and spent her days sewing, cooking, gardening, harvesting, feeding the pigs, and bathing in the river Ikva. She told me that for fun young people would gather to dance and sing in the evenings. Her description of village life always made me think of my summers at Ukrainian camp. It's a terribly romantic and simple vision of youth, nostalgia easily triggered by humid air or a well-timed firefly, the sky a gradient of deeper drowning blues, a single glint of star. It is youth and beauty distilled, a place with no other consequence besides these.

But perhaps simple places are always doomed to complication. Perhaps I am wrong and there is no place on earth without consequence.

Busia is afraid because of the village. The story I have pieced together is this: one month Soviet officials showed up in her region with orders to collectivize the local farmland. My grandmother's father refuses to go along with the decree. He was a patriot, proudly raising his babies to speak Ukrainian, though the area has been under Polish occupation for much of their lives. It was a daily struggle to raise Ukrainian babies and now they wanted to take his land, too. One afternoon there was a knock on the door. The authorities took my great-grandfather away at gunpoint. I imagine Busia was nearby, out back with the pigs maybe, or rolling *varenyky* dough in the kitchen. Knock, knock. She drops the roller and screams at the men who have her father by the collar.

A few months later a relative visited my great-grandfather in prison and that is the last time he was seen or heard from. Nobody knows what happened to the body, but almost 75 years later, I will find his name in the archives, under the title **Criminal Case № XXXXX.**

Bolsheviks bad men, Busia says matter-of-factly, as if we were talking about Cubs baseball. She pauses to stare at the mirror on the wall. *But father, he was good, hardworking man.*

What else do you remember about him? I ask.
Nothing. I not remember.

Because Busia says she does not remember, I am forced to imagine things. One time she was telling me a story about how, before her birth, her mother and father had to flee the village. There was a mass exodus, with most of the villagers leaving for Crimea. Meanwhile, Busia's family went to Lithuania to avoid the front. Her mother had been from Lithuania and so it was a natural place to stay for a while. When I asked which front it was (i.e., which war), Busia told me she couldn't remember. From my research I've gathered she was probably talking about WWI, when the German-Austrian front pushed toward Dubno around 1915. But she does not think of such events in grand historical terms. It is just what happened: They were taken. They fled. They left. We were taken. We fled. We left.

Because Busia says she does not remember, I make amateur calculations. Based on these, it seems her father was arrested by the NKVD (the KGB's precursor) prior to the arrival of the Nazi occupiers in 1941, and after the Poles had left in 1939. His arrest occurs, I assume, during that one fleeting year of Soviet reign—a sort of prelude to the long, dark night of Soviet reign that will eventually span from 1944 to the early '90s.

Busia's "bad men" Bolsheviks knocked on the door three-quarters of a century ago, but there is still doom and gloom in our weekly phone conversations. She spends much time reminding me of safety protocol and telling me that surely I am not eating enough, you need meat on your bones, how do you cook for yourself, do you eat out, who feeds you, you must be hungry as a wolf. At this point the discussion pivots from dour to absurd. I can't help but laugh while explaining to my grandmother that I live in walking distance from two grocery stores in Ohio and that I make all sorts of things like eggs and bacon, Caesar salad, pulled pork, and even *borshch*. I am very privileged, I tell her, to have such access to food. I am able eat all the time. And she is satisfied, at least for the moment.

Things lighten up after this. Besides danger, Busia is preoccupied with romance and my romantic life in particular. According to her, I am to find a *nice, tall, good-looking* man and that he should not, under any circumstances, be a Russian. A famous Ukrainian epic poem starts something like this:

Fall in love, you dark-browed maidens
But not with Moskali
For Moskali are foreign folk
They will not treat you right.

The word *Moskal* comes from an old name for the vassal state that had its capital in Moscow in the 1200s–1400s. A few hundred years after that, when the poem was being written, *Moskal* referred to members of the Russian army. Today, this Ukrainian word means simply Muscovites or Russians generally, and it is derogatory, a slur used mainly by Ukrainians, Poles, and Belarusians. It does not have a charitable connotation. (Its inverse equivalent is *Khokhol*, the name for a traditional Cossack haircut—completely shaved, save for a single long lock of hair on top. Today, *Khokhol* is an offensive term for a Ukrainian.)

The poem's protagonist, Kateryna, falls in love with a Russian soldier named Ivan. They have a steamy dalliance in the garden and Kateryna ends up pregnant. Ivan promises to return and marry her, but he never does. Now a lonely single mother, shunned and exiled from her village, Kateryna drowns herself in a pond, leaving her bastard son to wail and beg for the rest of his days. Later, Soldier Ivan will see his poor son panhandling on the street and though he recognizes the child as his own, he ignores him and rides off in his plush carriage. The poem's opening lines, written by Taras Shevchenko in 1838, will appear on a t-shirt printed by Ukrainian female anti-war activists in 2014. The lines will be accompanied by the slogan "Don't give it to a Russian" and an image of two hands in the shape of a vagina.

My grandmother recites whole stanzas of this poem by heart, sobbing into her palms: *Can you imagine, Sonechko? Can you imagine?* Busia tells these stories breathlessly, side by side. Soldier Ivan. The Bolsheviks. Ivan. Bolsheviks. It was never a stretch to couple Soldier Ivan with the men who took my great-grandfather, all of their uniforms stiff and line-dried, their black boots plodding, their intentions suspect. And so for a long time, this composite is how I imagined Russians.

+++

When I graduated from high school, my father took me on a long-awaited, much-anticipated trip to Ukraine. He and I would visit our relatives Marina and Yarosh in the village, but mostly we would just be tourists, stay in Western hotels in the major cities, eat at the best restaurants, sightsee, souvenir shop, inject dollars into the local economy and understand that we are being useful to someone. Diaspora families are always doing this.

My father bought for us what was, in 2007, the only English-language guidebook available for Ukraine. It was published by Lonely Planet, and the cover photo was of a castle, situated over a craggy cliff that dropped into what appeared to be a vast ocean. The castle had gothic windows, spires with flags, and princess balconies, all the whimsical features one associates with Disney, and the scene was filtered orange by a low sun. It looked majestic, but I didn't know then that the castle is actually a miniature, roughly the square footage of a small house. In the cover photo, there was no way to measure for scale.

I remember studying the picture and information inside—"The Swallow's Nest is one of several *châteaux fantastiques* located near Yalta on the Crimean peninsula"—and comprehending, perhaps for the very first time, that Ukraine had an entire border made of water. *Chorne More,* the Black Sea. Palaces and oceans must not have been part of my grandmother's Ukraine, or surely I would have heard about them. All I ever heard about were the pigs, the potatoes, the purling river Ikva. I was taken by the orange Swallow's Nest, but the idea of this bigger thing—the Black Sea—piqued my interest primarily because of how it might supplement our vacation: I was a teenage girl who wanted to lie on the beach and come home with a tan.

Tato, why don't we go to Crimea? I asked my father.

We don't want to go there, he said. *It's heavily Russified.*

So what?

Just trust me, he waved his hand, the way people do when swatting a fly.

I dropped the issue without a fight and didn't think about that conversation again until a few years later, around the time when this awareness started to emerge that our family was more afraid of something than other families—at least, it seemed, more afraid than the mostly white middle-class families that formed the periphery of my childhood. Or perhaps our family's fear was more specific. It was fear manifested as quiet contempt.

On that first trip in 2007, I bought a t-shirt from the souvenir vendors in Lviv's Vernisage Market. I slept in it every night for a month because it was so soft. I saw nothing wrong with the shirt, and neither, apparently, did my father. In large purple letters it read:

Дякую тобі боже що я не Москаль.
Thanks be to God that I'm not a Moskal.

+++

My attempts to assign more complex vocabulary to this phenomenon have not felt entirely fruitful. This isn't xenophobia, because after decades of occupation, oppression, murder, surveillance, a state-engineered famine, and the current ongoing invasion, my family's distaste for Russia isn't exactly *irrational*, as the definition suggests it should be. In Greek *xenos* refers to the strange, foreign, or unfamiliar, and that part isn't so cut-and-dry either. Though western Ukrainians especially tend to "otherize" Russians, it is also true that by most visible markers—culture, religion, physical attributes, lifestyle—the groups aren't so different at all. Both Busia and my father speak Russian in addition to Ukrainian. This is not a straightforward case of hating the unfamiliar.

Maybe bigotry is closer, but that term places special emphasis on opinions and ideas. Is it bigoted to dislike those who march through the world with imperial aims? Those who seem incapable of treating you without condescension?

Instead, it might best be characterized as enmity—"a very deep unfriendly feeling." The word enmity conjures up a hostility of biblical proportions: "I will put enmity between you and the woman, between your offspring and hers." In this analogy, the Russians are, of course, the dust-eating serpent. Enmity is a literary word, one that implies hatred left over from some long-ago circumstance. There is also an element of passivity. *It has been this way since before we were born. It has always been like this. This is part of us.*

Taras Shevchenko, the 19th-century poet who wrote *Kateryna*, meant the poem as an allegory. Soldier Ivan represents the Russian Empire, while Kateryna is the feminized, virginal, and subjugated Ukrainian nation. Shevchenko himself was born an imperial serf and didn't have his freedom purchased until age 24, when, interestingly, a Russian poet was able to use his influence in Shevchenko's favor. Luckily, Shevchenko was a talented artist.

Today Shevchenko is considered the father of modern Ukrainian literature and a useful national symbol. He remains highly venerated in Ukraine and his face appears on the 100

hryven bill. Busia and my father both have embroidered por-
traits of the mustachioed poet in their living rooms. Many
Ukrainians do.

+++

In the past few years, my effort to find language for our family's
particular brand of wariness toward Russia has been complicated by the fact that lots of people are talking about how we
ought to feel about Russia right now.

In 2015 I attended a Slavic conference in Ohio that hosted
academic panels on various aspects of Eastern European and
Eurasian politics, economics, and culture. The attendees were
mostly from Midwestern universities. The keynote speaker was
Karen Dawisha, a professor and prolific author on post-Soviet
affairs. She spent eight years researching her most recent book,
Putin's Kleptocracy: Who Owns Russia?, which was set to be published in 2014 by Cambridge University Press, the same house
that had published seven of her previous books. Once they got
a copy of the manuscript, however, Cambridge declined it on
the advice of their lawyers. They weren't concerned about the
quality of Dawisha's scholarship, but about political ramifica-
tions. "Given the controversial subject matter of the book and
its basic premise that Putin's power is founded on his links to
organized crime, we are not convinced that there is a way to re-
write the book that would give us the necessary comfort." New
York-based Simon & Schuster agreed to publish it instead.

Dawisha, however, didn't spend her keynote hour talking
about the "pre-emptive bookburning" scandal, as she calls it
elsewhere, or about how she was a secondary victim of Russia's
culture of fear. Rather, she used the time to talk about President
Putin and his closest friends.

Dawisha traced a few of the more notable and corrupt
friendships, the ones where Putin's old KGB and judo bud-

dies were designated to high-ranking political posts, or were granted astronomical construction contracts for the Sochi Olympics. While Dawisha relayed the hundreds of billions of dollars that have been stolen by the Russian government in various ways since the fall of the USSR, I could feel an energy spike in the room. When someone asked about how the Russian Orthodox Church was involved, she said that it was like the time of medieval indulgences, that you could "buy" anything you needed from the church, including a designated patron saint. In 2007, for example, the venerable St. Seraphim of Sarov was named the official protector of Russian nukes, both strategic and tactical.

That did it—all of us in the chandelier-vaulted conference room started laughing. It was quiet at first, like a wave pulling back from the sand, and then it gained strength. The idea that an ancient contemplative hermit whose most famous attributed quote goes something like, "Acquire a peaceful spirit and thousands around you will be saved," could be re-purposed by a violent authoritarian government in the age of nuclear weapons was both amusing and absurd. We laughed because we were smarter than them. We recognized the absurdity, and the Russians had to live it.

In fact, I can't account for the others in the room, though I can speculate. Undoubtedly some had Russian backgrounds and allowed themselves to see the humor in order to avoid being downtrodden by the gloomier realities. Others were Slavophiles, academics whose identities have been built upon a love for and fascination with Slavic culture and whose cocktail small talk benefits from being able to cite obscure facts like the patron saint of the Russian nuclear program. Whether directly or incidentally, all of us sitting in that conference room on that American campus had some dog in the not-so-distant fight for determining world order. When the Cold War era's bipolar system collapsed, the US emerged as a kind of de facto winner, at least according to our own metrics. And that dynamic is perhaps most troubling: we were laughing at an old enemy, the losing team. Russian corruption may be very real, but sometimes I think we are nearing *schadenfreude,* that we are guilty—that *I* am guilty—of deriving some twisted pleasure from Russia's absurdities, from the sheer horror of it all.

+++

On the second day of the conference, I attended a panel cohosted by my father who had traveled from out of town. He is a professor of political science, which is why even as a child I was never fazed when he said things like *heavily Russified.* That was simply how he spoke. I probably wasn't much older than 10 when he quoted Churchill to me, describing Russia as *a riddle wrapped in a mystery inside an enigma,* which is how I first learned what the word enigma meant.

Together my father and another local Ukrainian professor led a roundtable discussion on the ongoing Russia-Ukraine crisis. During his allotted time, my father mapped out the key points of Putinism and hybrid warfare, concepts he said were vital to understanding the conflict in eastern Ukraine. When asked by an audience member where he thought Putin was (at the time of the conference, the president hadn't been seen in public for over a week, and #PutinIsDead was trending on Russian social media), my father admitted that of course he himself had no clue, but Putin probably loved the attention. *He's notorious for being late to meetings because he likes people waiting for him,* my father explained. *Putin once made Angela Merkel wait for three hours, and she's the most powerful woman on the planet.* I will remember this comment three years later, when it is reported that Putin kept Donald Trump waiting in Helsinki.

My father is a highly methodical and confident teacher. As he advocated for Western assistance to Ukraine, I could tell that even the most skeptical attendees in the room found his argument compelling.

But if we arm Ukraine, one audience member with a British accent said, *then we're practically inviting Putin to send in more weapons. The violence will only increase.*

Well sure, my father said, relaxed and leaning back in his chair. *But it doesn't matter because Russia has already been engaging in warfare for months now, and they're just going to continue increasing their military presence and destabilizing the region—unless the cost suddenly becomes too high for them. Russians don't want their soldiers coming home in body bags either.*

Later that day, as I am leaving the conference with a friend, he seems to be doing a calculation I've never done myself. *Do you think maybe,* my friend begins slowly, *the reason you're so preoccupied with Eastern Europe is that your child-self is trying to get your father's attention? Like you're trying to get him to listen to you?*

The question feels almost accusatory. I resent it, but I am also challenged by it. No, it had never occurred to me that I might be seeking approval in some roundabout, Freudian way. The question surprises me and so does my answer. I do not expect the words that come next.

No, I tell him. *But you know how people talk about intergenerational trauma? Like how really intense trauma can somehow be passed down genetically? What if that principle applies to things like fear and passion, too?*

+++

I have never in my whole life thought about trauma in relation to myself. Owing to some combination of white, middle-class privilege and luck, I have moved through this life feeling as if nothing truly bad has ever happened to me. But when I said this to my sister once, she disagreed and brought up examples. As a teenager, I watched my beloved stepfather die of throat cancer. I came home after soccer practice one day to him on the bathroom floor, bleeding out from his stoma, and later, I would watch my mother sobbing over his corpse in the bedroom. Around this same age, I lost two high school friends and an uncle to suicide, all within six months, two guns and a noose, a small epidemic. And, of course, there are the everyday horrors a woman faces on the sidewalks of this world: cat calls, dirty words, the man stalking you on a bicycle with his genitals exposed, the time you were harassed by Belarusian police officers late at night.

These happened, and maybe they were traumatic, but they also occurred within the context of a rich support system. When I was a child, I remember adults often calling me *mature* and *well-adjusted*, words that seemed to confirm the idea that nothing had "gone wrong" with me, that I was developing exactly as they thought a child ought to. So speaking about trauma feels foreign and uncomfortable. The notion of transgenerational trauma was nowhere on my radar until the precise moment I was asked that question about my father. In that instant, my bloodline felt like the only honest explanation.

Although I may be something of a stranger to personal trauma, my grandmother is not, and neither was my grandfather. During the relatively short period of my grandmother's youth, her home village was shuffled between the hands of three occupiers: first the Poles, then the Soviets, the Germans, and the Soviets again. She and my grandfather lived on the front lines of a world war, the territory that historian Timothy Snyder calls the "bloodlands." It was there, sandwiched between Hitler and Stalin, that 14 million noncombatants of various ethnicities were killed in just 12 years. It is well known that approximately 6 million of those were Jewish Holocaust victims, while the rest included massacred prisoners of war, fatalities from state-engineered famines, and those killed in purges. There is much debate about the exact figures, and Snyder's book does not account for third-party violence during that time, such as the slaughter of Poles carried out by Ukrainian nationalists in Volhynia, or the retaliatory killings of Ukrainians by Poles. Snyder admits his number is "on the conservative side."

But Busia and my grandfather survived. I don't know how or why. They don't like to talk about it, which may be because they forget, or because they've willed themselves into forgetting. Both of them speak five languages, for example, and this was always discussed within the family as a point of pride. But how exactly they learned each one—Ukrainian, Polish, Russian, German, and eventually English—was not always so clear. I assume their survival is connected to these languages, to these five tongues purling around in their throat. I do not know much about how they came to America, but what I do have are these few fragments:

I. Busia is taken as an *ostarbeiter,* or "eastern worker," into Germany. She is a foreign slave from the occupied territories, shipped here to alleviate Germany's wartime labor shortage. A rich German family with children, a family loyal to the Nazi party, may qualify for an *ostarbeiter* nanny at a good price. A very reasonable price, really. A status symbol and a big help around the house. The state doctor shines a flashlight into Busia's eyes. He picks at her ears with a cotton swab. He notes the texture of her hair and marks its color on a chart. Holds a stethoscope to her spine. Busia passes the racial screening. Her Ukrainian peasant features are Aryan-looking enough for a home placement, which means the racial purity of Nazi Germany won't be terribly disrupted if the father of the household decides to rape my grandmother.

II. Busia is raising babies for a rich German family, a family loyal to the party. There are six children to rear, ages 10 to infant. Busia has learned German by now, the language of the enemy, and is a big help around the house. Maybe, like the other *ostarbeiters,* she is forced to wear a patch with the letters OST on her coat lapel at all times. Or maybe, her German family would rather forget that detail.

III. Busia tells me once about her brother-in-law, Vasyl, who grew up a bit farther east, in central Ukraine, where the Soviets were intentionally starving the Ukrainian population. Once, a fellow villager started chasing Vasyl, who was just a child at the time. Vasyl knew enough to be frightened. He ran and hid up a tree for several hours, the older man howling below, banging on the wood, Knock, knock, knock. Some in the village had already turned to cannibalism. The man was trying to eat him. *It wasn't so bad for us,* Busia says, after finishing the story. *Not so bad like that.*

IV. All the *ostarbeiter* nannies have been taken from their German homes and reassigned to factories. When I ask Busia what she made in the factory, she says, *I not know.* A part of a part, perhaps. A cog in a machine.

V. Busia is moved from one German prison camp to another. It is wartime and the frontlines are shifting and so camps must be consolidated. She is riding on a truck into the new displaced persons camp. My grandfather spots her from the ground and claims love at first sight. They are married in the camp. My grandfather's job is to pass out daily bread rations. Everyone is locked inside the camp walls, a guard posted at the gate. When Americans liberate the camp, they toss chocolate candies to the DPs. Busia and her siblings beg not to be repatriated, because back there, Stalin is still knocking on doors across the empire. Later, outside Chicago, my grandfather will get a job at the Wonder Bread factory. *This is the best country in the world,* Busia often says, meaning America.

VI. Busia is bulging with child. My uncle is a baby, tucked inside her. In 1949 they win the refugee lottery, and Busia's condition earns her a lonely airplane ticket. The rest of the family will come by boat, months later. Busia speaks four languages by now, Ukrainian, Polish, Russian, and German, but when she lands in New York City she does not speak this one. A Ukrainian volunteer meets her at the airport.

Are you hungry? the woman asks.

Yes, Busia says.

What would you like?

Borshch.

The woman laughs. *They don't have that here,* and she orders tomato soup for her instead. Busia has a remarkable memory for certain details.

+++

Much has been written about the transmission of trauma between generations, with studies indicating that the offspring of trauma survivors are more prone to developing PTSD than other groups. In discussing how and why the children of Holocaust survivors sometimes report horrifying nightmares of annihilation, clinical psychologist Natan P. F. Kellermann points to epigenetics. He says that epigenetics are typically defined as the heritable changes in gene expression that occur as a result of environmental stress, rather than from changes in the underlying DNA sequence. Severe trauma, he argues, leaves a mark on the chemical coating of the chromosomes. That coating acts as a kind of acquired "memory," carried and transmitted by the cell. A person's epigenetic characteristics don't necessarily determine behavior, but rather a predisposition to certain behaviors and responses.

Imagine this: It is a very normal day. You are milling about, doing your usual things. Something tickles your nose. You ignore it at first, certain that you must be imagining it. But the smell persists. It is sweet, like almonds or honeysuckle or summer jasmine. It is a pleasant smell, you think, until—*zzzzp!!!*—your toes are burning. Your leg muscles spasm, contracting and expanding without your input. The bottoms of your feet are raw. You have the feeling that a moment in time has dissolved, that it has skipped over you entirely. Where is it? Where am I? The smell dissipates and everything creeps back to normal.

Later, on a different day, you will get a small whiff of almonds and freeze. Your spine will go rigid. You wait for the tingling in your toes. You are afraid.

In a recent study conducted by Brian Dias at Emory University, researchers exposed mice to acetophenone, a chemical with an almond-like scent, for 10 seconds and then delivered a small electric shock. Predictably, the mice began to fear the almond smell. Less predictable, however, was how the mice's offspring also demonstrated a fear of the smell— though they never experienced a single electric shock themselves. The offspring mice in the study were born by way of *in vitro* fertilization to unrelated mothers, so they were not even raised by the parent who had endured electric shock. And yet, they were still terrified of the almond smell. These results held true for both the children and grandchildren of the original mice. The offspring were sensitive to the smell, stopping dead in their tracks, jumping at noises, acting nervous or startled. Memory of the experience had somehow been communicated genetically.

I wonder if Kellermann's concept of the epigenetic transmission of nightmares, or the sensitivity to smell demonstrated by Dias's mice, might be applicable to other phenomena as well. For example, could my father's distrust of Russia be a manifestation of something hereditary, of a fearful message first coated on the chromosomes of my grandmother? Do my cells signal Russia as the enemy? Am I somehow biologically more sensitive to the crimes of rogue states? Is our family's nationalist bent an acquired "memory," a passion developed, carried, and passed on for survival? Where does nature end and nurture begin, and in so often privileging the latter, do we miss something in the former?

Kellermann warns that with epigenetics "we should be careful not to slip from reasonable assumptions to fantastic and unsupported scenarios," which I know is precisely what I am doing. My theorizing could be construed as a cop-out, an excuse, a distraction from our family culture or some worse hidden prejudice. Yet, science is just now starting to commit to the idea that our epigenetic makeup may be a reflection of previous generations, a notion in itself so mysterious and convoluted that I can't help but entertain all possibilities, even if it means venturing briefly into the territory of the absurd.

After all, what are war, violence, and trauma if not absurd?

+++

I am friends with a Russian, a proper Moskal.

Ivan smokes too much, drinks too much, swears too much, and wears the cable-knit sweater his mother made him for several days in a row. He also hates Putin, which these days is a kind of prerequisite for educated Muscovites under 40, as he is. In fact, he hates Putin so much and has written so many articles criticizing Putin's regime that Vanya can't go home. He's been told that if he flies back to Moscow, he will be arrested at the airport owing to "public calls for violent change of the constitutional order" and "public calls for disrupting the territorial integrity of Russia" (i.e., for writing that Russia ought to return the annexed Crimean peninsula to Ukraine). So for now, Vanya is stuck in Ukraine, which is where I met him and where we became friends who liked to talk politics. He says that people have been nice to him there, that people are mostly just curious about what a Russian is doing in Ukraine while the two countries are at war. People have been friendly, and so he thinks "exile" sounds too dramatic, but that's technically what it is.

This happened once before, and, again, the word exile was not used to describe it. Vanya was 10 years old when he got an infection, possibly from a wet head or some bad combination of foods, he can't remember now. It was Soviet times. An official decided it would be best to quarantine him for two weeks in a hospital outside Moscow. In forced isolation Vanya couldn't see or speak with anyone, not even the medical staff. They put him in a private room, served food and pills through a small square hole in the wall with a door. He remembers they gave him lots of oranges to eat. He hasn't liked oranges since. Every few days the doctor's voice grumbled down from the intercom into his room, dispensing wisdom, telling the boy exactly what to do, what not to do.

His parents couldn't visit either. Once, in the middle of the night, Vanya wiggled through the small serving hole and into the hallway. He found a telephone connected to the wall and called his parents, but can't remember what he said to them. Come get me, probably. His mother figured out which window was his, but she didn't have a plan to break him out. Instead she wrote messages in the snow below: *Kak dyela?* How are you? He could only wave back.

+++

I am friends with a Russian officer named Ivan.

Before he was a journalist exiled in Ukraine, Vanya was a military man. He was conscripted to the Russian military intelligence agency (known as GRU—one of the agencies that will eventually be implicated for meddling in the 2016 US election) in August 2001, and a month later Putin welcomed 9/11 as the perfect pretext for enhancing his own hardline stance against Islamic militants in Chechnya. Just 10 years after the Cold War, America and Russia became unlikely bedfellows in the face of some elusive existential threat.

Since he had studied Arabic at university, Vanya's job was to listen to the intercepted phone calls of "known Middle Eastern terrorists" and translate whatever seemed important. We were sitting at an outdoor café in Lviv—I on my second beer, Vanya on his fifth—when he told me he had heard an Afghan man speaking with someone from the CIA over the cable that fall. The local Afghan was sharing Osama bin Laden's precise location. It was still 2001, just a few months after the Twin Towers, and Vanya rushed to his supervisor, told him that he knew exactly where bin Laden was. The supervisor frantically took the information to his superior, but nothing ever came of it. (Did I mention how Putin welcomed 9/11 as the perfect pretext for his own war? Did I mention that perhaps America also wanted a pretext?) I gawked at Vanya, unbelieving. I pulled a cigarette from his pack on the table, though I don't usually smoke. The waitress brought us a new ashtray. Somewhere, a calendar hung on a wall.

Maybe he made it all up, the story about finding bin Laden 10 years before the US government officially did. Sure, Vanya drinks too much and likes to talk too much. He is a storyteller. But then again, I don't know why he would invent this one. I am not able to reason it away.

Vanya finished his time with GRU and today is a journalist who hates oranges and really just wants to see his mother. He's been covering the crisis in Ukraine since it started, writing mainly for Russian speakers, trying to hack through the swirl of propaganda. He married a Ukrainian woman, though not for love or pregnancy or some more pious reason; they married for a mutually beneficial visa situation. Vanya once confessed to me that he thinks he does have a child somewhere, deep in the heart of Russia, but that he has no way of contacting the mother. Her family tried to reach him once, years ago, and the phone line went dead. Or maybe they hung up. He seemed quite sad about this, his eyes glassy for a moment. I wonder if somewhere there is a small child who, inexplicably, hates oranges.

After I left Ukraine and Vanya stayed, we talked on Facebook. This past year, it was mostly joking about the White House. Vanya called the American president "Comrade Trump" and professed his Russian love for Donald. He didn't mean what he was saying, but he said it anyway, delighting in the fact that now we too had a man of questionable morals in charge of our country, as if misery requires company.

I was back in the States in September 2016 when Vanya got banned from Facebook for three days (a significant length for someone who posts nearly 10 times a day). Indeed, there has been a flurry of banned accounts since the start of the Ukraine-Russia conflict. Ukrainians criticizing Russia and getting reported for it; Russians calling Ukrainians *khokholy* and having their accounts frozen. Ukraine's President Poroshenko even implored Mark Zuckerberg directly to create a different monitoring process for posts by Ukrainian nationals.

"Many people have been asking why I was banned," Vanya posted after being allowed back onto the site. "I was banned for the word which I proudly carry around in Ukrainian reality. The word—MOSKAL! That is, myself!" He called himself a Moskal on Facebook and got flagged for it. But in Vanya's control, Moskal cuts through the enmity. It casts a strange and uncomfortable light on hardened old borders. It makes the notion of a longstanding inherited feud sound silly. Ivan laughed at the Facebook regulators and concluded his post with the opening lines from Shevchenko's "Kateryna."

Fall in love you dark-browed maidens,
But not with Moskali,
For Moskali are foreign folk,
They will not treat you right.

Vanya has been alive for 38 years and some nights, after a few beers, he runs through languages as if they were all on the same flat plane. Arabic, Ukrainian, English, Russian. He is un-apologetic: as if borders and epic poems and sobbing grand-mothers and their KGB nightmares in Chicago suburbs don't matter. As if the absurd is just a fact of life and, beyond that, there are no rules.

+++

When my grandmother talks on the telephone, it is part folk science, part poetry, part proverb. *Don't call the devil,* she says to me because I am whistling while waiting for her to pick up the phone. In Ukraine, whistling inside the house will stir evil spirits. *Only on the street, Sonechko.*

I know, Busia. How are you?

I'm fine, she sighs. *No good news, no bad news. I have arthritis, sciatica, my back hurts, but I still keep living. Are you eating?* I picture her sitting on that box in the kitchen, beige cord snaking up her bare leg and crisscrossing its varicose veins.

Yes, Busia. I'm eating. Some days her question irks me, but most often I manage to find it amusing. I am privileged, I know, to take eating for granted.

Ty holodna yak volk? Are you hungry as a wolf? She wants to know if I am starving. Today, she uses the Russian word for wolf.

No, Busia, I'm fine. I eat all the time.

Ok, fine, she breathes heavily.

I promise, I say.

How is my car? Busia says, changing the subject. She is talking about her silver 1994 Dodge Spirit, which she gave to me when she decided to quit driving. The rooftop is rusting, but the vehicle has shockingly low mileage, as it traveled only to Divine Liturgy on Sundays and to different neighborhood grocery stores, chasing the weekly sales on eggs and milk. A Ukrainian *tryzub* coat of arms dangles from the Spirit's rearview mirror.

It's running great, I tell her. *I love it so much, Busia.*

That's good, she says.

So, what did you do today? I ask.

Busia launches into the plot summary of the latest Shevchenko poem she's been reading. In this one, a boy, Marko, learns that the woman who had been the family maid is actually his biological mother. The woman is on her deathbed when she reveals her true identity, leaving Marko no time to react before she is dead.

Busia says she and some other Ukrainians did a live performance of this poem called "The Servant Girl" back in the displaced persons camp in Germany. But when she tells me about it, her voice is fast and eager, as if she just encountered the story yesterday.

Marko faints and when he wakes up, mama dead! she relishes the drama.

That's sad, I offer.

Yes, it's tragedy, Busia says, heavily now. *Marko lived whole life with his mama in the same house, and he didn't know it. He didn't know where he come from.*

I will agree a few more times, while Busia, in the mood for poetry, asks about my love life. It doesn't matter what I answer because she will always respond with the same advice. *Remember,*—for this, she switches entirely from Ukrainian to Russian—*lyoubov ne kartoshka, ne vybrosish za okoshka.* Love is not a potato, don't throw it out the window.

After Busia and I say goodbye, I sit at my own kitchen table and stare at the nook above the sink. That's where my portrait of Shevchenko hangs. The painting is on a slab of circular wood, almost two feet in diameter, with geometric folk designs etched around its border. The piece was given to me in Ukraine and now serves as a topic of conversation for dinner parties in Ohio.

When my friend gave it to me, I thanked him and meant it, but privately wondered how I would ever bring something so bulky back home with me. I had traveled to Ukraine with only one suitcase and it was already full. Plus, it was kitschy, I thought, only to be appreciated in the context of some irony. I made secret plans to re-gift the impractical portrait and avoid the hassle.

But the day before my flight, I changed my mind. I caught Shevchenko looking at me, his forehead rutted in thought, his gaze stern. I bought a duffel bag at the market and cushioned his solemn face with socks and sweatpants. It felt profane to leave Shevchenko behind. Even if I'd wanted to, I'm not sure I could have.

INSTRUCTIONS FOR PARENTS IN UPBRINGING CHILDREN
(1950)

I. Explain to children that Russians are not our older brothers, and neither are they our guardians or liberators. Russian Bolsheviks are enemies of the Ukrainian people; they are exploiters and oppressors!

II. Explain to children that the Pioneers, Komsomol, and other Bolshevik organizations can harm our people; they want to brainwash our children, make them obedient tools in the hands of our enemies—the Bolshevik Party. Their aim is to separate us.

III. Don't trust the Bolsheviks, avoid them at all costs. Young adults must not become close to or marry a Bolshevik.

IV. Don't speak Russian, don't greet each other in Russian or Bolshevik style.

V. Explain to children what damage and crimes the Bolsheviks are perpetrating against the Ukrainian nation.

VI. Teach children how to act in Bolshevik schools.

VII. Explain what Bolshevik propaganda really means.

DUCK AND COVER

Busia keeps a calendar in her kitchen, above the garbage can, beside the toaster. It hangs across from the mirror. It is always a free calendar, a calendar that her Ukrainian credit union mails to each of its members. The pictures are idyllic folk scenes: a leaf resting on a lake, the entrance to a forest, a basket of bread, a sunflower field. In the boxes below Busia marks significant dates in half-English, half-Ukrainian. A birthday, a name day, a death day. Orthodox custom demands attention to detail, and so these dates must be tended carefully. On the 3rd day after a death, for example, we pray that the deceased will rise as Christ did. On the 9th day, we pray for them to join the nine choirs of angels. On the 40th day, we mark the soul's final departure. The calendar, then, looks like a cemetery map, each name a small tombstone in time.

When the Chelyabinsk meteor hit, it was winter and so my grandmother's calendar probably showed a cozy hearth, or a ski hill, or a wooden church shrouded in snow. The credit union calendar scenes do not hint at possible destruction, but instead evoke fertility, tranquility, domesticity. The calendar offers one kind of truth, I suppose, though it is not the whole truth. Actually, there is only a single fact to rely on here: when the meteor hit, I was in a place where the meteor was not hitting. Everything else we know is difficult to verify.

I. Sasha, student, age 8

The main difference between me and you—besides that I am a teacher and you are a student—is that on the morning of February 15, 2013, I was in a place where the meteor was not hitting and you were in a place where it was. I was learning how to command attention at the chalkboard, and you were tucked under your desk. Though I am a teacher, I am not your teacher, and that is a good thing. I wouldn't have known what she knew. My instincts have not been trained like hers. She came of age alongside the Atom. She was born on high alert.

Duck and cover is what your fourth-grade teacher screamed, but what she meant is this is war. Her drill was left over from one long-gone cold, from when old men cast us as enemies. You did as she said, huddled low and hoped the long-gone drill would work because there was a rush of light 30 times brighter than the sun inside your classroom. *Jesus Christ what is happening?* The children. The calendar. The windowpanes clanging like incense burners. *Woe is me! Lord have mercy!* Clang. *Deliver me!* The calendar. The children. Clang. *Pilot my wretched soul, do not despise thy servant, count me worthy . . .* Thank God for that teacher because if you had been outside, little Sasha, you would have retinal damage and winter-month sunburns, white banks making a reflection of a reflection of the star in your eye. In the enemy country where the meteor was not hitting, it was cloudy.

When the meteor hit, infrasound waves cracked glass all over town, but not in discernible patterns. Your second window on the east side, your fish tank, French doors, the mirror for your father and his morning shave. Like many of the local men, your father is probably a veteran of Chechnya in the 90s, which would mean he's seen it all, seen places turned to powder under presidential orders. You are small, Sasha, so all you see is the vodka now, but your father was probably there in uniform, in Grozny, when the UN named it the Most Destroyed City on Earth, which is almost but not quite giving credit where credit is due. (*The Army, which had been diminished under Yeltsin, was henceforth to be reborn . . .*, Russian journalist Anna Politkovskaya wrote.) Your father, he's seen it all, so on the morning commute when the sky exploded above his automobile like the day of fiery reckoning he said, with absolutely no emotion, *Damn.* We know this from his dash cam.

After school you, little Sasha, will wade through Siberian snow to search for black gold. You'll follow the drift-holes to dense rock below. You are an expert at digging for the stones because your hands are small and, in your excitement, you easily forget the cold. You'll search for hours, beg your mother to postpone dinner. Soon, strange men in dark cars come to cruise your village. They will idle in front of your house and offer thousands of rubles for the fragments your small hands fished out of the yard. There is a black market for natural shrapnel.

A few weeks later, in science class, after they have fixed all the windows, your teacher will tell you about meteors. As she speaks, your teacher's eyes will lose focus, only for a second, and perhaps no one will notice but you. Her eyes drift idly toward the calendar on the wall, its blue-yellow-red numbers. She searches for some significance, her thoughts like a runaway tank. *Meteor, asteroid, comet* . . . Even after the lesson, you are still not sure how to draw a meteor. Maybe it is a mountain, balled up, rolled like dough. Maybe it is like your mother's *pelmeni*, stuffed with expensive gravel. Maybe a meteor is a million gravel-stuffed dumplings all held together with fire, which is difficult to imagine since you haven't yet learned how to count to a million. You attempt to draw this anyway.

Nine months later, scientists will take the biggest stone for themselves, drag it from the bottom of a lake nearby. A 1,442-pound close shave, your father thinks to himself as he admires your *pelmeni* meteor on the fridge. No one is home. The refrigerator hums in the background. He rips off a chunk of bread and floats toward the couch, grabs the remote like a gun. Takes aim.

People can consider February 15th their second birthday, your television governor says, but what he means is victory can happen to anyone.

II. Yelena, hospital orderly, age 41

We are nothing alike because I am not a mother. I have never had to wave goodbye to a child leaving for school, have never crossed myself thrice for his safety, or prayed he would look both ways at the intersection by the post office. I have never needed to protect anyone, save myself and my own soft belly. I am not a mother, and so all I can say about pain is that I, too, sometimes cry at the sight of a sunflower field.

Officially, there never was a rocket. It never landed anywhere and certainly not in a sunflower field in Ukraine, the faraway country next door. (. . . *the necessary background and scenery for a dirty little war,* Anna Politkovskaya wrote years earlier of Chechnya.) I was just leaving the next-door country as your son was arriving. We passed in the night like trains, like lost tanks. I was just leaving Ukraine as your son was arriving, though officially, he was nowhere.

A zinc-lined coffin travels better through air and x-ray machine, so they hermetically seal your son like cucumbers and slaw, like the cellar of jars you've saved just in case. Sauerkraut.

Beets. Last year's pig. He looks up at you through a small window in the coffin top, cheeks sallow. Instant army noodles aren't enough for a growing boy, you think, angry all over again, wondering why you hadn't called his commander sooner to tell him that growing boys need meat. The commander has never crossed himself thrice for your son's sake. The commander has never needed to protect anyone, save himself.

You, Mrs. Yelena, will not be able to sleep. Every hour you startle yourself awake by lunging at the calendar. At first you want to kill it, shank it with your kitchen knife, but later you settle for counting and recounting the boxes. *August 10, August 11, August 12* . . . You sob and accuse the page of conspiracy. You fold the corners into complicated patterns that only you can remember. (*More and more, it seems to me that each of us has our own personal calendar,* Anna Politkovskaya said.) You check again tomorrow for evidence of tampering.

There was no rocket, but when it landed, your son was somewhere in Ukraine, 500 miles from Chechnya where they told you his Rifle Brigade was permanently stationed, and 900 miles from your Volga Basin home and the couch where he should have been sleeping. You lie awake on that couch all night, asking yourself why you weren't there, what you could have done differently. *Duck and cover* you remember from the old days but your son is so young—20, a barely stubbled baby face—he didn't know the drill, hadn't seen it all. If you had been there, you would have covered him with your own chest, with your pale back, with the soft, sagging part of your stomach. If you had been there, beside him, chin-high in a field of sunflower faces. You would have looked at him and seen yourself.

Now, you barely feel anything. There is a notarized death certificate (*multiple shrapnel wounds to lower limbs, acute massive blood loss, origin not established*) and a son who used to have legs. There is a secret funeral you're not allowed to tell the relatives about. Tears freeze to your face. The coffin is shrouded in snow. You fuss over a bouquet of plastic dahlias because, in the absence of a crowd, you must find another way to make this pile of dirt significant. You fuss over the floral arrangement and then cross yourself three times. No, not three times, but thirty times three.

Back on the couch you wait months for your television news anchor to mourn with you, but she never mentions your son's brigade or the sunflower field across the border. You cradle the remote like a baby, dumplings growing cold on the plate beside you. The refrigerator hums in the background. Men in uniform float before your eyes, and you reach for them.

Russian paratroopers make history today by landing on a drifting Arctic iceberg where they will practice survival training, the anchor reports, which is to say there is no war, but if there were one, we'd be winning. Which is to say, all targets are moving.

III. Anna, journalist, age 48

I want to be as brave as you, but I'm not yet. I stay up all night reading your books about Chechnya, about the horrors you witnessed and the people you tried to protect by screaming truth into the giant vacuum that is your motherland. The authorities hate you for your words against their dirty war.

I am a pariah, you say.

I do not matter enough to be anyone's pariah, I think.

I sleep with your books under my pillow and pretend we are having conversations, like an interview in reverse:

What shoes did you wear in Chechnya?

In Chechnya, twin baby girls were killed before they learned to walk.

Would you have hung your granddaughter's artwork on the fridge?

Right now I have two photographs on my desk of people who were abducted.

What do you dream of?

Faint explosions were heard and a silvery-violet, tulip-shaped column of smoke appeared.

Do you still cry or have you forgotten how?

Mass poisonings at schools in the Shelkovsk region.

Are there any pomegranate trees left?

The Army continues to rage in Chechnya.

What are you most proud of?

I am not one of his political opponents or rivals, just a woman living in Russia.

I am outside on a street. It is night in Moscow. I have never been to this place in waking life, but I am here now. The building in front of me is made of old stones. There are two tall wooden doors and a blue mailbox to the left. The building is at an intersection, and there is a street sign tacked near the corner: 8 Forest Street. A few people pass on the opposite side of the road. They push a stroller with a balloon tied to the handle. They do not notice me and are gone after a minute. There is also a man. He is dressed in black, a black cap on his head. He is beside me, waiting in front of the building. I look into his eyes and see my own reflection. I can't say where he ends and I begin.

This man knows the building code, ####. He gingerly pulls open the tall door and snakes inside. The stairwell is dark and damp, a bag of potato chips and a juice box rotting in the corner, a condom wrapper, a pile of dead, wet leaves. It is October. The hallway walls are painted in typical Soviet fashion: a coat of thick blue up to your neck. It is hard to leave fingerprints on this paint. It is a good method for keeping the communal hallways clean, for cleansing them of unsightly human oils. All the old *kommunalkas* have halls in this color. It is a color that conspires to say, *everything is alright.*

He hangs outside the elevator, tucked behind a pillar of steel. Water drips in the corner. A fuse box hums. The man stands there, haunted as a tree, leaves twitching, fingerprint grazing the trigger. He waits. And waits some more. Somewhere, a baby is born.

Inside the elevator doors, there is nowhere to duck. A close range CRACK-CRACK-CRACK, like timber. A round of hellfire from a handgun shot by a hit man as random as the weather.

Ms. Anna, what is the definition of a war? When you wrote that the state was targeting *enemies who needed to be "cleansed,"* is this what you meant? Is a hallway also a battlefield?

The elevator opens to your crumpled body, a bag of groceries wilting on the ground beside you. Your long, limp legs, broken glasses, the gray hair behind your ears whispering, *I've seen it all.* The only explanation is this: four shots, one to the head, and a standard-issue Makarov pistol. Killer unknown. You will be mourned on Forest Street and in the country next door and around the globe. You will be called brave and people will point to your articles, to the time you were abducted by federal troops. Another time you tried to save 1,000 hostages—children, in fact. On a southbound airplane, on your way to negotiate their release, the flight attendant served you a cup of tea. Forest fruits. You woke up in a hospital, a nurse bending over you, whispering about poison. All official blood test records have been destroyed. There is a black market for good reasons to go to war.

Your friends and family will grieve the loss of an almost-grandmother because your daughter was pregnant that night of the elevator. Your granddaughter will be born in the spring and they will name her Anya, like you. She will learn to walk, and ride a bike, and draw stick figures for a family and spell her name while the authorities pretend to be looking for the murderer. On the day of the elevator, you had been shopping for a tub in which to wash your almost-granddaughter. You promised to stop going to Chechnya, to stop writing about such awful things just as soon as she was born. Maybe, when baby Anya is grown enough to know this story, she will get caught in a hailstorm one afternoon. She will get caught on the way to work wearing her best dress and shoes. Sopping wet and sore, she will cock her soft face to the sky and wonder about luck. She will wonder where she came from.

Three days after the elevator, it is your funeral. You are due to be buried in Troyekurovskoye Cemetery, which means everything happens in threes, life is a troika. Thousands of people walk by your coffin, leave their tears on the inner lining. They present you with flowers. The priest lays a white paper band across your forehead, according to the Orthodox custom. It is printed with the Trisagion, the thrice holy prayer, *Holy God, Holy Mighty, Holy Immortal, have mercy on us.* It is not so much a band as a crown. You wear a crown into the ground to signify your victory. Your maiden name, Mazepa, came from your father's Ukrainian side. Whenever a Russian heard you were from the ancient Mazepa clan of royal Cossack warriors, they would shrink in fear. Your father kept a library of banned books. You were a warrior, too, and this printed paper your victory.

Ten years later, when my own grandmother dies, I will admire her crown of glory and think about where I came from. I will gaze at her sunflower face, which is another thing she used to call me: *sonyashnyk*, sunflower. Standing there over my grandmother, I am a reflection of a reflection.

Thousands attend your funeral, but not the television president. He calls it a *disgusting crime*, and then qualifies his statement, saying, that in fact, Anna Politkovskaya's impact on Russian political life was *extremely insignificant.* I wonder what your granddaughter will think when she hears this. Is it really such a silly thing, to feed and wash your daughter's daughter?

A crime of vile brutality should not remain unpunished, the president proclaims after the elevator, but what he means is it's time to party: today is my birthday, and the car is waiting out back.

+++

You are a saint, and I am not yet brave enough. I don't know how to give my whole life. I forget to call my grandmother on holidays. I have not raised any children, only this pathetic little troika. Can you forgive me? For that day, I was in a faraway country. For that day, October 7th, was my birthday, too.

WORD PORTRAIT

(underline all that apply)

1. **Height:** tall (171–180 cm), very tall (over 180 cm), short (155–164 cm), very short (up to 154 cm), average (165–170 cm).
2. **Figure:** stout, full, medium, lean, thin.
3. **Shoulders:** raised, lowered, horizontal.
4. **Neck:** short, long, noticeable, protruding Adam's apple.
5. **Hair color:** blonde, light brown, dark blonde, dark brown, black, graying, gray.
6. **Eye color:** blue, gray, greenish, light brown, brown, black.
7. **Face:** round, oval, straight, triangular, pyramidal, diamond-shaped.
8. **Forehead:** high, low, straight, sloping, protruding.
9. **Eyebrows:** straight, arched, meandering, wide, narrow, fused.
10. **Nose:** small, large, thick, thin, wide. Nasal bridge: bent, straight, convex with a hump. Nasal base: raised, horizontal, lowered.

11. **Mouth:** small, large.
Corners of mouth: turned
down, <u>turned up</u>.

12. **Lips:** thin, <u>thick</u>, sagging
lower lip, raised upper.

13. **Chin:** sloping, <u>straight</u>,
protruding, forked, with
a pit, with transverse
groove.

14. **Ears:** small, large, oval,
triangular, square, round.
Protruding ears: upper,
lower, general. Ear lobes:
fused, separate, inclined,
angular, oval.

Special features: none

VESELKA

There is a place that does not exist yet. It may be black, or a color we cannot imagine, or no color at all. It goes on forever in every direction. In the center (can there be a center?) is a golden egg, gilded and burning. The egg is wrapped in nothingness like a royal bathrobe. I don't know how the egg got there.

It is even harder to describe what happens next, for there is some kind of clock left unaccounted for in this place that does not yet exist. An alarm, a time bomb, tick, tick, boom. The golden egg cracks from within. There is a god in there. He is called Rod. Later, we will use his name to describe ourselves: *narod* (people), *rodyna* (family). But today, in this place that will soon exist, Rod sloughs off the broken bits of shell, like birthday confetti. He looks about, sees how the oceans and seas are mixed up with the sky, and understands that he has a lot of work to do. No one can survive in such chaos. He begins to move, but wait!—there is a problem. Rod is attached to the egg. He gropes about in the nothingness. He hits something: a bow. It is frighteningly sharp. Seething, razor-sharp. Rod doesn't want to have to do this, but he sees no other way. The tie must be severed. It has to be slashed. Rod cuts his umbilical cord with a rainbow and goes about creation.

+++

My Ukrainian grandmother is dead. I am standing in Busia's Chicago-area kitchen, having flown here last minute. My plane circled her neighborhood before landing at O'Hare, where my uncle picked me up from the terminal in his sleek, black Jeep.

Busia's kitchen feels dead. It doesn't smell like onion or boiled cabbage or anything at all. Busia has not been here for weeks. She has been dying at a facility where people go to die in America. Before she went to the facility, she was not cooking much for herself. Instead, my uncle would bring large packages from Costco: giant trays of shrimp cocktail, pre-mixed greens, meatballs, salmon fillets with lemon slices. Everything was delivered in plastic containers, and so at the end, it all slid cleanly into the dumpster.

I am standing in Busia's kitchen in the embroidered *vyshyvanka* blouse I have decided to wear to her wake. Using the mirror above the microwave, I tug at the *vyshyvanka* wrinkles, strategically tucking them into my black skirt. I adjust my Orthodox cross necklace—one Busia gave me off her own neck while she was dying—and hide the clasp under my hairline. I've always appreciated the extra bar at the bottom of the Orthodox cross. A footrest for Jesus. Or, if he felt like it, a way to jump off. I smooth my brown fly-aways and the single silver strand mushrooming up from my part. Someone offers to feed me, but Busia is dead, and I do not have an appetite.

+++

The most famous Ukrainian kitchen in the world is located on the corner of Second Avenue and East 9th Street in Manhattan. It's difficult to measure a thing like fame, but regular people in Ukraine know about this restaurant in New York and 3,000 *varenyky* (pierogi) a day seem as good a measurement as any. They sell for nearly $2 each, which is scandalously high by Ukrainian standards and wholly un-scandalous by New York's. Busia—who occasionally visited an all-you-can-eat buffet, but otherwise preferred to cook for herself—would have found the prices at this restaurant unforgivable. The most famous Ukrainian restaurant in the world sells a $17 plate of *holubtsi* (stuffed cabbage rolls) and *bigos* (kielbasa stew) for $18, both of which you would be hard-pressed to find for more than a few bucks in Ukraine.

The place has a storied history, serving as a favorite haunt for artists, writers, and runaways in the East Village of the 1960s. Penny Arcade, a performance artist who first started frequenting the restaurant in 1967, recently told the *New York Times*, "It had the *Village Voice* before anywhere else, a row of phone booths, smokes for a dime and cheap good food that never changed." The restaurant has played host to movie productions and celebrity diners like Jon Stewart and Parker Posey. Today, the old world-inspired dishes are served on white plates emblazoned with the restaurant's neat logo and name in a clean, hip font: **Veselka, EST. 1954.** *Veselka* is the Ukrainian word for rainbow.

+++

Actually, in my mind, Veselka is not the most famous Ukrainian kitchen. It is not even the second most famous. My list goes like this:

1. Busia's kitchen in Chicago, IL
2. *Oselia* kitchen in Baraboo, WI
3. Veselka restaurant in New York City, NY

For much of my life, Busia's seemed like the only Ukrainian kitchen in the world. I split my childhood between my mother's house in South Dakota during the school years and Busia's house during the summers. I did not know any Ukrainians in South Dakota, and so Busia's world felt like an island.

Kitchen #2 existed in a place that was like a very small island off the coast of another island. An islet, perhaps. Between the ages of 8 and 14, I attended Ukrainian soccer camp every summer. This is exactly what it sounds like: a weeklong camp at the beginning of August for children of the Ukrainian diaspora who like playing soccer. But even more than the soccer, I liked just being there, in the leafy woods of Wisconsin, surrounded by other American kids whose grandmothers fed them blueberry *varenyky* for dessert and who forbade them from whistling inside the house. At camp, our English was braided with the vocabulary of a pre-war Ukrainian village, and we didn't have to explain ourselves. At camp, my name felt effortless.

The camp is owned and operated by the Ukrainian Youth Association, a scouting organization often referred to by its Ukrainian language acronym, СУМ, or the Anglicized, CYM. Every summer since 1961 CYM members flee from Chicago to the Wisconsin campground *oselia*, a word that means roughly settlement or dwelling. I, too, vacationed each summer on the Wisconsin *oselia*, where my father's family and their diaspora friends had been vacationing for decades.

At camp our schedule was rigorous. We awoke at 7 a.m. to the shrill of a whistle and a commander yelling, *Vstavayte! Get up! Vstavayte! Dobroho ranku! Good morning!* The commander led us in group stretches and push-ups before we were dismissed to get cleaned up, prepare our barracks and tents for inspection, and march down the hill for morning assembly. We stood at attention, cold dew licking our toes, for the flag raising ceremony—both Ukrainian and American flags—while singing together "Shche Ne Vmerla Ukrayina," the national anthem. We recited the "Our Father" in Ukrainian, and "Bozhe Velyky," another hymn that seamlessly combines religion ("God is great") with patriotism ("Give Ukraine strength and glory, freedom and power").

After morning announcements, we proceeded to the converted barn where middle-aged women in hairnets served hot plates of *varenyky*, eggs, sausage, and Styrofoam cups of tea. I noticed that some of these women had strong accents, which as a child gave me the sense, however vague or unfair, that there was some sort of loose hierarchy based on one's temporal distance from their US arrival. I recall a camp friend making fun of a Polish woman's lip liner once, calling her a "stupid immigrant."

Between mealtimes, we practiced soccer for several hours a day, swam in the pool (an enormous Ukrainian *tryzub* painted on its floor), and played card games in the grass. At night we told flashlight stories and sent scouts from tent to tent to inform fellow campers about who had a crush on whom. In this respect it was not so unlike your typical American summer camp: the strangeness of shaving your puberty-ridden legs in a shower hung with spiders; the freedom from your parents' nagging for seven days straight; the intimacy of an inside joke among young girls; the nervous thrill of holding hands at dusk and the outline of Alligator Mountain fading before your eyes. But more importantly, *his* eyes—blue and yellow mixed together, swirling tie-dye eyes. This teenage boy smells incredible there, beside you, his Chrome Azzaro cologne. He is drenched in it, almost pickling. He smells incredible, like flowers and bacon and rain and the way nostalgia makes your stomach feel. In the future, when you are grown and moving through the sidewalks of the world, you will catch a whiff of Chrome Azzaro and be flung violently back to those hills. But right now he smells so incredible you are not thinking of the future. You are not thinking of the past either, or of the rock you've perched on to watch the sunset behind Alligator Mountain, which is actually a memorial rock. It is marked in memory of the millions of Ukrainians (three to four million perhaps, though the exact figure is unknown and widely disputed) who lost their lives in the Soviet-engineered famine of 1932–33, called the Holodomor (hunger-extermination) and recognized by seventeen countries as genocide. You are so busy kissing the bacon-rain-tie-dye boy that you forget about the genocide.

At camp I was concerned with the stink of my soccer cleats and the new Missy Elliott CD playing on repeat in the girls' tent. I was in love with the hills and how I didn't have to explain myself. I was so in love that after my first year at camp, I remember clipping my toenails and saving the clippings in a small, secret box. Every so often I would open the box and cradle the trimmings. At camp, these were part of me. They touched that grass and those hills. If a scientist could test them, I thought to myself, they would find my DNA and the DNA of the *oselia* grass, both together! After cradling the nail crescents, I gingerly closed the box and tucked it high on my bookshelf.

At camp I was concerned with my soccer cleats. I was not concerned with the origins of CYM, or the project of Ukrainian nation-building, or even the fact that my father and uncles and cousins had attended camp here, too, and that Busia had, at one time, worked in the *oselia* kitchen. Only as an adult would these historical details start to assume meaning. Youth, instead, is lived as reaction, as instinct.

CYM, the Ukrainian Youth Association, has thousands of members spread across roughly nine countries, from Belgium to Argentina. Its objectives are written on the organization's website:

    I. To organize, nurture, and educate youth in the spirit invoked by the ideals "God and Ukraine."

    II. To form Christian and patriotic values as well as morally sound individuality.

III. To cultivate the unity of Ukrainians around the
world.

IV. To work for the good of the Ukrainian Nation and to
strengthen its statehood.

As a child, I did not consider these objectives with any serious-
ness. What does a child know of state sovereignty? But today
I find myself pouring over these details, as I would have once
studied the recommended beauty products in *Teen Vogue*.

CYM officially attributes its founding to a Ukrainian university student, Mykola Pavlushkov, who, in response to the
encouragement of his uncle, began an underground youth organization bent on resisting the Soviet regime. The organization was interested, allegedly, in restoring private property and
reestablishing a free Ukrainian state. CYM's website invites you
"to put yourself in the shoes of 18 year old Mykola. To organize an underground organization, in a country controlled by
a totalitarian military regime [is not a simple thing] . . . Even
taking into account an 18 year old's fearless idealism, this was
a step that could only be undertaken by a courageous person
with truly extraordinary convictions."

And Pavlushkov's convictions were suspect. It was the late
1920s, and the Bolsheviks were already tired of their short-
lived policy of Ukrainization. In the eyes of Moscow authorities, Ukrainian patriotism could not be properly controlled and
any manifestation beyond brief ceremonial use of the language
or a kitschy appreciation for, say, *hopak* dancing was far too
dangerous. In 1930 Pavlushkov was arrested and put on trial in
Kharkiv, alongside 44 other Ukrainian intellectuals including
three women, two Jewish men, and several academics charged
with founding the Union for the Liberation of Ukraine (SVU),
the parent organization to Pavlushkov's youth association. According to CYM's account, Pavlushkov and the others were
found guilty of planning terrorist acts, a crime that fell under

Article 54 of the Criminal Code of the Ukrainian SSR. All of them died either in prisons or concentration camps, including Pavlushkov, who was executed at Solovki gulag camp seven years later.

CYM's origin story is iconic and inspirational, but it's also a bit misleading. According to the *Encyclopedia of Ukraine*, the 1930 trial at the Kharkiv Opera Theater was a show trial, and CYM and SVU were fictional organizations, dreamt-up by the Soviet authorities as a pretense for persecution. The Soviets fabricated their administrative structures and "appointed" their leaders, with Pavlushkov named head of the fictitious youth branch. He and the others were indeed arrested and killed for being members of the Ukrainian intelligentsia, well-versed in Ukrainian literature and language, and thus natural proponents of Ukrainization. (One state report cites how Taras Shevchenko's poetry was being used to inspire a counter-revolutionary uprising.) It's unlikely, however, that the accused were in fact participants in a single underground movement.

By leaning into this pseudo history, CYM is using the same falsehood once used by their Soviet enemies, albeit for different reasons. Instead, it would be more accurate to say that CYM, which today exists and operates around the world, was established *in homage* to Pavlushkov and the other victims of the show trial. CYM, as I know it, was started in 1946 in the displaced persons camps in Germany. It was started by those who had lived through Polish repression, Soviet aggression, and the brutal German occupation. Those who desperately needed to revive and protect their Ukrainian heritage in the midst of so much tyranny. It was started by people like my grandmother.

But when I was at soccer camp, I didn't care about the history of CYM. I cared about whether my clothes stayed dry.

It is one of my later years as a camper, maybe 2001 or 2002. The older girls and I sleep on cots in an army tent, a sweeping mass of canvas and poles. We call our home the *shatro*, an old Ukrainian word that means a tent, but which also implies something grander. It is the tent of the Old Testament, the dwelling of the tabernacle. *Shatro* is a holy tent.

Our *shatro* is made of thick flaps. It is dark green and smells ancient, like a leftover from the war our grandparents fled. It is stifling. On a humid August afternoon, the tent is a trap. Do not be deceived by its shade. Inside the canvas tent, the temperature is always 20 degrees hotter. It reeks of sweaty shin guards and teenage cleats.

I am sleeping on a cot under the big-top of a repurposed army tent. It is the middle of a summer night in Wisconsin. Mosquitos, cicadas, a box fan humming from the barracks. It is loud out here, but also quiet. I am exhausted from hours of soccer. I sleep soundly, until it's too late. There is a single drop on my pillow. Drip. A small stream on my pillow. I roll my face into the wetness. My cheek. I blink. Dark figures are stirring on nearby cots. I stare up at the black canvas. *Oh shit,* someone grumbles. There is lightning, thunder like artillery. Everyone is awake now, cursing the sky. I throw on Adidas sandals and drag my cot into the center of the *shatro.* The walls are rushing waterfalls.

It is not a normal summer downpour, but a small flood, one we will talk about for years to come. The girls and I slip and slide on rivers of grass outside the *shatro.* The sky flares above. We run, screaming and giddy toward the bathroom. The toilet floors are cold cement, their corners occupied by mean bugs. We perch on a wooden bench and spend the rest of the night beneath the bathroom's fluorescent lights, singing and laughing and complaining about how our shoes will be soaked. Did I leave my socks hanging on the line? Blades of grass stick to my calves. Mud sunk into the beds of my toenails. It is accidental camouflage.

At camp, I cared about rain.

+++

Busia is dead in a box. The lid is closed now, but inside she is wearing a *vyshyvanka* to match mine and an Orthodox crown of glory. *Holy God, Holy Mighty, Holy Immortal, have mercy on us.* I spin the clasp of my cross backward. The sun is glaring on our Ukrainian section of the Chicago cemetery, where Busia is to be buried between her husband and her youngest son, only a few paces away from her sister, her brothers, and her mother.

One of my cousins is wearing sunglasses to hide his crying. Another cousin is wearing his father's suit, a bit too roomy. Another cousin wears a priest's collar and pulls a small jar out of his pocket. It is soil from Nina's ancestral village, he explains to the mourners. Nina was always insistent on keeping strong ties to the old country. He offers the jar to my uncle and father. They sprinkle the dirt onto Busia's casket. It is that same fertile dirt that earned Ukraine the reputation as "breadbasket" of Europe. That famous, fertile dirt that made the 1932–33 Holodomor famine an especially cruel irony. That famous dirt that put the conquest of Ukraine at the center of Hitler's "ideological colonialism," as historian Timothy Snyder calls it. "Had Hitler not had the colonial idea to fight a war in Eastern Europe to control Ukraine, had there not been that plan, there could not have been a Holocaust." Snyder continues, "because it is that plan that brings German power into Eastern Europe where the Jews lived."

We scatter the village dirt on Busia, and then walk toward our sleek cars. Like all good dirt, it is mostly composed of dead things.

+++

Kyiv is a city of hills sliced in half by the Dnipro River. Overlooking the river, on top of one of the highest hills, there is a neon rainbow. Start here. Understand that this rainbow only looks like a real rainbow at night. During the day, it is the color of steel. Under the rainbow, there are several figures cast in bronze and granite, all men, all of them giants. Two of the giant men hold hands. They are a Russian worker and a Ukrainian worker. They are good Communist workers. Other giant men are doing business. They are signing a document. The Ukrainian Cossacks are pledging their allegiance to the Russian tsar. These giants are as wide as 300 years of history.

The People's Friendship Arch monument opened in 1982 on the 60th anniversary of the October Revolution, which also happened to be the 1,500th anniversary of the founding of the city of Kyiv. The monument is dedicated to the unification of Ukraine and Russia. From up here, you can see the ex-president's Spanish ship, the white beach at Trukhaniv, and the Breshnevki apartment blocs that spike like teeth from the left bank. Up here, you can see almost everything.

From the Arch, you also have a nice view of Podil neighborhood, one of the city's oldest and the birthplace of its commerce and industry. Podil's historic buildings curve with the right bank of the Dnipro. Its name, *podil,* means lowland. It is a flood plain. For much of the 19th and 20th centuries, this was where the Russian authorities allowed Jews to settle.

The Great Choral Synagogue is here in Podil. It was Kyiv's first permanent house of worship for Jewish residents and the only one to remain functioning in the post-war years. It is a bright red building, white window trim as intricate as cake frosting. During the war, the German army used it as a horse stable.

If you pass through Podil to the west, you'll go by the grounds of the old Zaitsev brick factory where Menachem Mendel Beilis once lived and worked. Beilis was a Jewish man accused of the "ritual murder" of a 12-year-old Russian boy in 1911. Two lamplighters said a Jew had done it. Beilis sat in prison for years awaiting trial, while the prosecution played with the evidence, twisting and turning public opinion. At trial, the lamplighters admitted they had been played with, too: vodka, poured by the tsar's secret police. Beilis was acquitted. But do not dwell on this—Beilis left for America years ago. He is long gone.

Past the brick factory, northwest just a few kilometers from the synagogue, there is a park. There aren't many cars here. It is a retreat from the horns and shopkeepers and sirens of Podil. The park is lush and purring. Mosquitos, cicadas, distant traffic humming like a box fan. It is both calm and noisy. Both quiet and loud, like a long soundless scream. The park is where a ravine used to be. Now, it is a hill. It is a mountain of corpses covered in dirt. This park is Babyn Yar, which means old woman's ravine.

> No monument stands over Babi Yar.
> A steep cliff only, a crude headstone.
> I am afraid.

I first learn of Babyn Yar from a Russian poet with a Ukrainian last name. My family does not speak about Jewish Ukraine, about tens of thousands of corpses thrown into a yawning ravine. No, we try not to look down there. I am sitting in a Catholic high school classroom in South Dakota. I flip through our English textbook and there is a Ukrainian name. Right there, in our American textbook, in South Dakota! The name is attached to a poem. In the poem, I read of an unfamiliar Kyiv. This Kyiv is not part of my family's tour.

Start at the People's Friendship Arch. Trace a line up and over through Podil, up and over through the brick factory. End at Babyn Yar. Notice how you've made a bow.

+++

I was living in Lviv, Ukraine, when I first saw the article online about Baraboo, Wisconsin. "Monuments to Ukrainian far-right movement erected in US." Someone must have posted it on Facebook, though I can't recall for sure how I found it. At the time, I was three years out of college and had not visited the Wisconsin *oselia* in seven or eight. I had become more interested in books and traveling and politics and less interested in playing soccer. I had mostly lost touch with my old camp friends, save for an occasional happy birthday text message from the boy with the blue-yellow eyes. I had not actively severed any ties, but they were out of sight, tucked on some high shelf, not easy to reach. I was less prone to romanticizing those green hills and that small flood. They were good but distant memories.

My work in Ukraine was all-consuming, until—"A group of monuments to Ukrainian nationalists has been set up in the US city of Baraboo in the Sauk County, Wisconsin." I saw the article, published on Voice of Russia, a Kremlin-funded news outlet. It had the look of an early HTML site with bright blue hyperlinks. "Several bronze busts of Symon Petliura, Yevgeny Konovalets, Roman Shukhevich and Stepan Bandera, all members of Ukraine's 20th century violent independence movement, have been erected on the territory of the Beskyd summer camp, which belongs to the Ukrainian Youth Association (CYM)." And there was a photo. A shining green hill, the same hill at which I stood every morning to sing and pray in Ukrainian. At the base of this familiar hill were four unfamiliar pillars. Atop each pillar a golden bust, all stern-faced and short-haired. They looked like brothers.

I vaguely recognized all of the names, but it was the last one, Stepan Bandera, that gave me pause. Bandera was born in what is now Western Ukraine. During the 1920s the region was still under Polish rule, despite the League of Nations urging Poland to give Ukraine national autonomy. Instead, Polish authorities closed Ukrainian schools, abolished Ukrainian professorships, censored newspapers, and barred Ukrainians from participating in the political sphere. The Poles even opted to use the term

"Rusyn"—which has a more provincial connotation—than the modern word "Ukrainian." Busia explained village life in Western Ukraine matter-of-factly: *We go to school, they make us speak Polish, then we go home and speak Ukrainian.*

While the Poles were repressing in the West, Bandera was also aware of atrocities committed against Ukrainians in the East. In 1932–33 the Soviet authorities manufactured famine conditions by seizing grain and murdering Ukrainian peasants who attempted to keep or consume their own harvest. (The authorities were starving people in other parts of the empire, too, Kazakhstan in particular, though I did not learn this until much later.) Stalin's Five-Year Plan intended to jumpstart the collectivization process and rid the USSR of one of its more economically and ethnically problematic groups. Accounts from the Holodomor are the stuff of horrible nightmares. People burying potato skins, hoping they'll grow. People eating leaves and worms. People eating excrement. People eating their own children after they died. On Thanksgiving one year, I remember Busia whispering the story of great uncle Vasyl, how he climbed a tree to save his life. I imagine the starving man, hungry as a wolf, howling up the trunk. Busia shrugged, *Everyone is hungry.*

Against this backdrop, the Organization of Ukrainian Nationalists (OUN) was growing, with Bandera as a prominent young member. (Konovalets, one of the other golden busts, was elected as its leader.) OUN wanted justice for a repressed Ukraine, but they wanted it at the expense of nearly everyone else. Bandera and his fellow nationalists envisioned a free and sovereign Ukraine governed by Ukrainians. They were not concerned with granting rights to ethnic minorities, and so Bandera's vision was a dangerous and narrowly nationalistic one. OUN set about its work by assassinating high-ranking Poles, Soviets, and even Ukrainians who compromised with these outside forces.

When WWII began the OUN resistance viewed the Germans as perhaps their only hope for defeating their oppressors, avoiding further Bolshevik rule, and gaining autonomy. Though the Ukrainian nationalists and the Nazis had different and distinct aims, the echoes between them remain deeply unsettling. It was an ugly collaboration, fueled at least in part by the historical conflation in Ukrainian popular consciousness of Jewry with Bolshevik rule. The conspiracy theory of Jewish Bolshevism alleges that the Russian Revolution of 1917 was orchestrated primarily by Jewish activists. Although several Jews did hold prominent positions in the early days of the revolution, they had also endured life in an empire riddled with anti-Semitism and pogroms. It is not surprising, then, that some individuals may have found hope in the promise of communism, though many Jews suffered tremendous repression under Stalin as well. In the years since the October Revolution, the notion of Jewish Bolshevism has been blown up and used to justify more anti-Semitism. Hitler himself cited the "annihilation of Jewish Bolshevism" as a goal worth achieving with every ounce of strength and fanaticism.

When German armies invaded the Soviet Union in 1941, some contingents of OUN fighters and followers of Bandera marched alongside them, though Bandera himself was not in Ukraine at the time. That summer the newly formed OUN police assisted *Einsatzgruppe C* carry out multiple pogroms against the Jewish residents of Lviv. (One of those pogroms was undertaken in the name of Petliura, the first of the golden-bust brothers.) The pogroms are, of course, the stuff of most horrible nightmares. Jewish residents beaten and kicked by restive mobs. Women stripped naked and paraded through town. A Ukrainian man dressed in a traditional *vyshyvanka* shoving the face of a Jewish man against a Lenin statue, forcing him to kiss it. Killing lines, stacks of bodies. When I first heard the news about the golden busts in Wisconsin, I was walking those same streets in Lviv that Jewish families had been made to scrub with toothbrushes.

When the Nazi troops moved into Ukraine, the OUN used the window of chaos to declare a free Ukrainian state, promising it would continue to "cooperate closely with the National-Socialist Great Germany, which, under the direction of its leader, Adolf Hitler, is creating a new order in Europe and the world and helping the Ukrainian people to escape Moscow's occupation." It is almost laughable now, given the wide view afforded by our historical distance, to think that Hitler would have ever been interested in such an arrangement. After all, he had appointed Erich Koch as *Reichskommissar* of Ukraine precisely because Koch hated Slavs. "If I find a Ukrainian who is worthy of sitting at the same table with me," Koch once famously said, "I must have him shot." Despite the OUN's apparent willingness to cooperate, Hitler demanded that the Ukrainians withdraw their proclamation of statehood. The OUN leaders refused, and so the Germans detained prominent members of the group and had Bandera brought to Berlin and put under house arrest. He was later transferred to Sachsenhausen concentration camp. While he was in the camp, Bandera's followers took to the forest and formed the Ukrainian Insurgent Army (UPA) to continue fighting the Germans, Soviets, and remaining Poles. (The fourth bust, Shukhevych, served as an UPA general.) Over 100,000 Ukrainians died fighting for liberation, liberation that, at least for some contingent of fighters, still assumed a menacing, nationalistic bent. As Timothy Snyder writes in *The New York Review of Books*, "In their struggle for Ukraine, we see the triumph of the principle, common to fascists and communists, that political transformation sanctifies violence." The Red Army ultimately triumphed and Ukrainians would endure more decades of cultural and political repression. Bandera remained in exile and was assassinated in 1959 by the KGB in Munich.

The busts are still there, four bronze foreheads glowing in the summer heat. I stare at my computer screen, mouth open as a gate. I am shocked that the campground of my youth—of teenage crushes, of Missy Elliott, of soccer stats, of lip gloss and new razors and blueberry *varenyky*—has attracted the attention of what is so clearly a Russian propaganda website. That it has become politicized. Was it always political?

I learn from CYM's website that in 2013 they held a dedication ceremony to bless the new memorial on *oselia*. The weather is beautiful and it is a large crowd in attendance. The president of the local CYM branch gives a speech about the four historic figures installed on the hill. *All four were murdered by Russian Bolsheviks whose goal was to destroy Ukrainian freedom, suppress the Ukrainian independent nation, erase the distinct Ukrainian identity from the face of the earth, and make Ukraine a part of greater Russia.* The CYM president is a tall and serious man, his uniform neatly pressed. *We want our children who come here to camp, summer or winter, to know the history of our heroes. To understand why it was so important for them to sacrifice their lives so that Ukraine may one day be free.* There is one mention of Nazi cooperation, which I am oddly relieved to hear. *Ukraine's conflicts with two totalitarian regimes: Communists and Nazis, former partners, yet in the eyes of Ukraine still united through an identical ambition of conquering Ukraine.* Campers hang floral wreaths on the four pillars. The color guard holds the Ukrainian flag as well as the red and black flag of the OUN. *Glory to Ukraine!* I admire the green hillside, which now appears to have a man-made waterfall running between the statues. This is another new addition. *Glory to her heroes!*

I begin to daydream about other busts. I wonder what different faces might look like there against the hillside. A bust of Alla Horska, perhaps, the dissident painter murdered by the KGB in 1970. Or the smooth forehead of Volodymyr Ivasyuk, the songwriter last seen in KGB custody and found hanging from a tree in 1979. Or Tanya Chornovol, the corruption reporter beaten nearly to death during Maidan.

Why not a bust of the unnamed Ukrainian man, from the same region as Bandera, who hid a Jewish woman in a garage during the Nazi executions? He had been delivering beets in his cart that day. When the shooting stopped, she asked if he might transport her out of town. The unnamed man agreed, quickly fetching a Ukrainian *vyshyvanka* for the woman to wear, and fled with her on his beet cart.

+++

It is Busia's funeral luncheon, and I am killing time in the women's restroom. A stranger introduces herself. She is the wife of CYM's president. *What a beautiful young lady,* she says, as we are washing our hands. *We are all so proud of you.* I did not know that Mr. and Mrs. President were family friends, though apparently they are. Mrs. President takes me to meet her husband.

They are a handsome couple, Mr. and Mrs. President, well dressed, soft spoken, and kind. I find their words of condolence very moving. They are so impressed by the woman I've grown to be. They are here to support my uncle and father but also to honor my *babusya's* legacy within the Ukrainian community of Chicago. She was a good woman. Not many are left from her wartime generation. As they are speaking about my grandmother, it occurs to me that I really do want them to be proud of me. I wonder if I would have grown to be the same woman without them, without CYM, without those few glorious weeks of not having to explain myself. That is, had I not first gone to *oselia*, would I have gone to Ukraine? Had I not sung "Shche Ne Vmerla" in the cold dew each morning, would I have been ready to sing it on Maidan? I thank Mr. and Mrs.

President through watery eyes, before proceeding to find my seat at the table.

My cousins and I get drunk at the funeral luncheon. The spread is imposing: long white tablecloths, salad, breadsticks, three kinds of pasta, pork chops, chicken cutlets, endless dessert, an open bar. All the funeral guests are dressed to the nines and the waiters wear cufflinks. One of my cousins and I begin planning a hypothetical trip to Ukraine, but settle instead on a third gin and tonic. It feels like a wedding, and we are at the head table. We are happy, almost. My father's second cousin tells me how much I look like my mother these days. *Did you even know her?* I ask. (My parents have not lived in the same state since their divorce.) *Of course,* she nods, as if there is a whole history I am unaware of. My cousin jokes that every Ukrainian funeral is Groundhog Day. The same funeral home. The same church. The same motorcade. The same section of the cemetery. The same Italian restaurant. The same game of who-is-related-to-whom-and-how. The same hangover. At some point in the afternoon, I start to cry.

After the funeral, I return to Busia's empty house where I will sleep in her bed before my flight the next morning. I spend the rest of the night watching old home videos, my grandparents twirling in their finest clothes, my father and uncle riding tricycles on the sidewalk. The video technology is so old that the footage has no sound. All of the scenes are soundless. There are several long shots from *oselia* in the 1960s, many minutes of silent, sweeping panoramas from other dedication ceremonies and prayer services. The young scouts—my father's generation—are sweaty and restless in their uniforms. The golden busts will not be erected for another 50 years, but the hills are there. The hills are green, and gorgeous, and screaming.

+++

Prior to WWII, an estimated 20 percent of Europe's Jews lived in present day Ukraine. Lviv alone had some 130,000 Jewish residents. When I lived there, I didn't meet any Jewish people, save for one or two visiting scholars from America.

I did, however, eat dinner at a "Jewish-themed" restaurant in the center of town. It is called Pid Zolotoyu Rozoyu (Under the Golden Rose) and is adjacent to the territory of what used to be the Golden Rose synagogue. The synagogue was Lviv's oldest until its destruction in WWII. The modern day restaurant, opened in 2008, is operated by a local Ukrainian company whose owner claims to have "studied Jewish history for three months." The place is cozy, with crocheted tablecloths and Klezmer music playing in the background. But when I saw the waiter wearing a black hat with fake payot sidelocks, my stomach sank. He invited me to try it on for a photo. I declined. When we got the bill, there were no prices listed, as apparently it is Jewish "tradition" to haggle and bargain after the meal. The restaurant deals in kitsch, non-kosher food, and anti-Semitic stereotypes. Perhaps it's also worth noting that the place never seemed busy. When I walked past it—which was often—the waiters were usually standing outside, smoking cigarettes with bored, blank faces.

The same company also operates an UPA-themed bunker restaurant just a few blocks away. In order to gain entry to that restaurant, diners must swear to the uniformed doorman that they are not Moskali. In return, the doorman will give you a shot of vodka from his army canteen. I spent Easter night 2014 drinking with friends in this brick bunker surrounded by images of Bandera and a collection of toy guns. Just a few weeks prior, we watched Putin illegally seize Crimea and blame Ukraine's politicians for being modern accomplices of Bandera. *Crimea will be home to representatives of all the ethnic groups that reside in it, but will never belong to Banderovtsy,* he announced from a television screen. What Putin didn't announce from the screen, of course, is the fact that, for the past several years, the Kremlin has been supporting far-right parties in Europe, including France's National Front, Italy's Northern League, and Germany's AfD, which won 12.6% of the vote in 2017, making it the third largest party in the German parliament. Far-right politicians in Ukraine, meanwhile, secured only around 3% of parliamentary seats in the 2014 election.

But who is Bandera anyways? For Ukrainians, he is an anti-Soviet warrior. For Russians, he is a convenient pretext for anti-Ukrainian policies, including invasion and annexation. He is a Nazi whose brothers died in Auschwitz. He is a fascist. A boogeyman. A hero. A myth. He is a violent fanatic who, as a university student, was known for sliding pins and needles beneath his fingernails, preparation for future tortures he might have to endure.

I do not know who Stepan Bandera is, but what I know is this: In 2006 a magazine published by a fringe university in Ukraine featured an article questioning Menachem Mendel Beilis's innocence and his acquittal, though he had been dead for 72 years. In 2014 two Molotov cocktails were reportedly thrown into the courtyard of the Great Choral Synagogue in Podil. And, for many years, it has been difficult for Kyiv city officials to keep spray-painted swastikas off the memorial at Babyn Yar. In the gray light of morning, when city traffic picks up like wind, four red spikes appear on the stone. They are evil, seething weeds, grown under a camouflage of nighttime. They have razor-sharp points and are very hard to wash off.

I do not know who Stepan Bandera is, but what I also know is this: In 2017 a vandal desecrated a Holocaust memorial in Rivne oblast. Ukrainian students from the nearby technological college who heard about the incident went out to the site that very day, got down on their knees, and scrubbed.

+++

In the move, everyone was accounted for. The fat dog with no spleen. The cat with a crunched up face. The rabbit with a silver feeding tube. The pigeon that flew backwards. The horse skeleton, the human skeleton, the monkey. A lady made of leather brought up the rear of the procession. When the German coroner moved, it was like unloading the Ark, or maybe it was the resurrection.

Dr. Edward J. Messemer, the deputy coroner of New York City, lived at 144 Second Avenue. In 1884, when Messemer decided to move down the street, the *New York Times* reported on the objects of curiosity filing out of the townhouse. He had a large private collection of bones.

But the Germans would begin to leave the East Village in the early 1900s, swapping places with a wave of East European Jewish immigrants. Philip and Benjamin Menschel, Jewish brothers from Austria, purchased the building at 144 and opened a movie theater. The building would become famous in the 1930s when a group of robbers dubbed the East Side Boys shot a detective inside the restaurant. Various shops, cafés, and offices moved in and out of the building. For a few months during the Great Depression, the Communist League of America—an opposition party accused of Trotskyism—had its headquarters on the third floor. From there, they published *The Militant,* a newspaper whose first issue warned in bold font of "the Right danger."

In 1954, a Ukrainian immigrant named Wolodymyr Darmochwal had saved enough money from his janitorial job to rent the corner storefront from the Menschel brothers. Darmochwal and his wife Olha had been forced to flee Ukraine during the war and had just come from the refugee camps in Germany. Maybe the same camp as my grandparents, though I can't say for sure. Darmochwal opened a small shop called Veselka where he sold coffee, cigarettes, candy, and Ukrainian-language papers. By 1964 the East Village neighborhood was thoroughly

Ukrainian and the Menschel brothers were looking to sell. The New York City branch of Plast—a rival Ukrainian youth scouting organization but with similar educational goals as CYM ("To be faithful to God and Ukraine")—purchased the building from the Menschels. Plast's headquarters remains there today, just above Veselka, which is now a 24/7 diner. Veselka serves chic Ukrainian fare (those $17 *holubtsi*) alongside Jewish specialties like gefilte fish. Considering the historical demographics of Ukraine, it's no surprise the cuisines have cross-pollinated. Darmochwal, for example, was close friends with Abe Lebewohl, owner of New York's famous kosher Second Avenue Deli. Veselka and the Deli opened the same year just one block apart. Darmochwal was originally from Ivano-Frankivsk oblast in Western Ukraine (as was Stepan Bandera and the unnamed man with the beet cart); Lebewohl was from Lviv oblast. When Lviv fell under Soviet control, Lebewohl's father was condemned for being a business owner. He was arrested, while Abe and his mother were deported to Kazakhstan. After the war they were allowed to return to Lviv, but all the Jews they had known there were gone.

I imagine Abe and Wolodymyr standing together on the corner of Second and 10th, chatting about the weather or the price of meat. They are looking outward, watching people cut through the small sliver of park on the opposite side of the street. There are certain things they don't talk about. Certain things, between them, that don't need explaining. The traffic here is loud, but they have both gotten used to it. After Abe's death in 1996, that tiny triangular park will be named in his honor. In the center, a memorial flagpole from 1944, dedicated to the victims of WWII by the Ukrainian American Society, "in memory of their sons."

I first visited New York in 2000, when I was 12 years old. The trip was my father's idea, and for months leading up to it he had been talking about Veselka, a Ukrainian restaurant that apparently even celebrities liked. My father didn't tell me about the

German-Jewish-Communist-Ukrainian history of the building at 144 Second Avenue, but he did tell me that Julianne Moore liked their *borshch*.

We went in the middle of the afternoon, after climbing into the Statue of Liberty's crown. I remember it was bright outside the window, the menu was paper. I ordered *varenyky*. Some with potato, some with blueberry for dessert. They tasted familiar. I couldn't believe it—Busia's food was here, inside a real restaurant in the biggest and loudest city I'd ever seen. Ukrainian food had always been confined to the *oselia* dining room or to Busia's retro kitchen. I didn't know it could exist outside of those two places, places far too personal to hold any significance beyond myself. I didn't know our food had consequence.

The name Veselka bows on the window. Did you know that every rainbow is a full circle? From where we stand on Earth, we just can't tell.

+++

On the night of Busia's funeral, after the luncheon and the silent home movies, I look around her house. I pick things up: small figurines, old pill cases. I blow the dust off and set them back down, exactly as they'd been. In later months, I will keep some for myself—a pair of shoes, an embroidered pillow, a headscarf—but tonight I am only looking around. I am breathing in mothballs like incense. It is too soon to disturb the house of the dead.

On the night of the funeral, above the coat closet, I find a bowl of *pysanky*, traditional Ukrainian Easter eggs. The eggs are red and brown and black with accents of yellow and orange, the colors arranged in geometric folk designs. To make traditional *pysanky*, you use hot wax to write on raw eggs. *Pysaty* means "to write." During Soviet times, *pysanky* were outlawed, like religious *samizdat*.

Behind the bowl of *pysanky*, tucked beneath a bouquet of fake flowers and other tchotchke—so high above the coats you couldn't possibly see it from the ground—I find a framed portrait. It is the face of Stepan Bandera.

Several months after Busia's funeral, while I am writing about Bandera, I dream of our Wisconsin *oselia*. It is my first camp dream in many years. I am there with the boy whose eyes look like a swirling Ukrainian flag. We are sitting on a green hill with some of our other camp friends, watching a soccer match. It is lush and humid and the hills are buzzing with bugs, and I am so glad to be back. I am remembering how much I love this place. But after a moment, I realize the hill we are sitting on is creeping. It is a bed of snakes. I love this place, and I am worried about what the snakes will do to this place I love. We must acknowledge the snakes. I suggest we put the snakes down in the gulley below, but my camp friends panic. That's where the other animals are kept, they say. We cannot move the snakes down there.

And my camp friends look at me like my suggestion is a betrayal. Like I have double-crossed them. Like I am the wickedest creature of all.

+++

Rod is a god of fertility. He crashes about the new world, eyeing its chaos. He aims to organize it. To say to the sky, *you belong there*. And to the sea, *you belong there*. He gives birth to order, a direction of life.

Rod is chiefly concerned with bloodlines, with the extension of clans. His egg has just cracked open. Outside, the new world is black or colorless. It is chaos, pandemonium, a seething, empty place. He breathes in nihilism like mothballs. The air itself is nihilism, though that word cannot exist yet. Rod aims to organize. To say to the family, *you belong*. Rod is concerned with bloodlines and so he makes a people with lineage. A clan must have a history, he reasons. A bloodline must have direction. He cuts his umbilical cord with a razor-sharp rainbow and goes about creation.

But my family never believed in Rod. We lived after the time of ancient Slavic gods. Busia was Orthodox. Orthodoxy meant icons and incense and crossing yourself thrice. Busia did not believe in Rod, but in Christ Resurrected. She believed in redemption. She believed in the legend of the *pysanky.*

There is a young Jewish woman from the Gentile town of Magdala. Her Christ has been crucified, nailed to a piece of wood, as casual as a curtain, hung for the crowds to look through. On the first day of the week, this woman decides to visit the tomb and anoint his body. She wraps precious oils and places some eggs in a basket. She might get hungry. The eggs will be an easy repast, a luncheon after the funeral.

She arrives at the tomb early, while it is still dark. Outside the tomb, she sees the stone has been moved. The hulking boulder, gone. Her instinct is to run. *Help!* she thinks. *They have taken my Lord.* But she pauses for a moment there, at the tomb, in the soundless, screaming dark. She lifts the cloth from her basket. The eggs are still inside, but they are no longer white. The eggs are the color of rainbows. They are every color—tangerine, raspberry, lime—and the brightest are red. Red as an open wound. A red ravine.

How can she hold a repast with the dead missing? And what of these strange colors? Could she scrub the red off if she tried? Should she run for help?

She looks at the tomb. Then at the eggs. She looks back at the tomb and at the eggs again. Tomb, eggs. She turns from the tomb and takes off, sprinting down, down, down the dusty hill. Beneath her feet, it curls like a skull.

ARTICLE 54 OF THE CRIMINAL CODE OF THE UKRAINIAN SSR

(1927 & 1934)

54-1 a—betrayal of the Motherland;

54-1 b—betrayal of the Motherland by a serviceman;

54-1 c—assistance by family members of a serviceman to flee abroad;

54-1 d—failure to report a planned betrayal;

54-2—armed uprising;

54-3—being an accomplice to the enemy;

54-4—assistance to the international bourgeoisie;

54-5—inciting a foreign state to declare war against the USSR;

54-6—espionage;

54-6 a—transferring inventions or innovations of state defense abroad;

54-7—subversive activities;

54-8—terrorism;

54-9—acts of sabotage of transport, communications, or water supply systems;

54-10—anti-Soviet propaganda and agitation;

54-11—participation in a counterrevolutionary organization;

54-12—failure to report counterrevolutionary crimes to the authorities;

54-13—counterrevolutionary activity during tsarist times or during the civil war;

54-14—counterrevolutionary sabotage.

SAMIZDAT

I. *The Land of Green Plums,* Herta Müller, 1993

When I am reading about the green plums, I am in the Black Hills of South Dakota, the land of ponderosa pines. I have never seen a plum here, although they may exist. The only native fruits I know are small, desperate berries. I assume anything larger than a chokecherry is imported.

That summer in Dakota everyone is worried about our ponderosa pines. The mountain pine beetle has arrived, and it is turning our forest brown. It is killing every tree in sight. Someone tells me the infestation is from Colorado, and I want to believe them, though later I will read that this is not quite true. The pine beetle was here all along, hiding among us. That summer I am spread on a blanket in the backyard, reading about green plums, while the trees around me are dying.

Herta Müller's universe is 5,500 miles and three decades away from my Dakota. Her characters are in Romania, living under Nicolae Ceauşescu's police state, a communist dictatorship. They are university students who become dissidents, young people who read the dictator in every village tree because they are paranoid, but also because he is there, haunting all the limbs. Müller's language, even in translation, is hypnotic, paratactic: The narrator's father says green plums are dangerous, will make you go crazy. Local authorities gorge themselves on the unripe fruit. The streets are so quiet you can hear chewing. The proletariat makes things no one needs: tin sheep, wooden watermelon. Grass grows inside your brain. It gets cut when you decide to speak. An exclamation point after a greeting is normal, but a comma means your life is in danger. Having a cold means you are being followed. Nail clippers are an interrogation. Everything sounds silly.

When I read about Müller's student dissidents it is summertime and the sun is hot, so I take the book outside to an old army blanket spread beneath the ponderosa pines. It is 2011, the summer before I will move to Belarus to teach at the country's largest state university in Minsk. George W. Bush famously calls Belarus "Europe's last dictatorship," but some political scientists say he is wrong, that it is not exactly a dictatorship. It's true that in Belarus there are no free elections, no free press, and no separation of powers. Alexander Lukashenko has been president for 25 years, but his is still not a totalitarian regime. His reign enjoys a certain degree of public consent, the analysts say. It is not as bad, not as wholly oppressive as it could be. Over 50% of Belarusians still work for the state, but at least now there is a McDonald's and a Nike store. Today's Belarus does not make you speak in code. It is not Ceaușescu's Romania.

But the summer before Belarus, *dictator* is the loudest word, the one I hear most clearly. I am enamored with the sound of it, the danger of it, the raised eyebrows when I tell people *I am moving to a dictatorship*. I am charmed by the weight of history and adventure and resilience in its three hard syllables. If it is possible to carry something like a word, then this is the one I take to Minsk.

I arrive in August, in time for the academic year. I begin teaching English but feel like every class is anthropology in disguise, like my students and I are studying each other through language. I am an eager researcher, but not always a good one. I project Müller's characters onto my students, as if all young people at state schools in so-called dictatorships are the same. After classes, I gorge myself on experience: A bombing in the metro. The worst inflation rates in the world. Cookies with worms in them. Women tricked into ballerina bodies and sex tourism. Radiation fallout, blowing north with the wind, full of state secrets. Co-workers pointing at the ceiling when what they mean to say is *our president*. Jokes told over cognac.

I am gluttonous. I eat these tiny poems and try to digest them. Independently, the images are silly, meaningless, but taken together I am convinced they are hieroglyphs, signs directing me up to Lukashenko, to the dictator. I can barely contain myself because I think I have figured it out, that I have cracked some code, and that I must share my findings. I publish an essay on a US-based travel website. I don't make a conscious decision to mimic Müller, but I am doing it; my language is paratactic and cryptic. When the essay goes live I think that surely no Belarusians will ever find it, much less read it. They are not the audience for this US-based travel website, I reason. I am also young, and I take it for granted that writing is art and not politics. That writing can bring you to sighs or to tears, but that it will not bring you to jail.

> When we don't speak, said Edgar, we become unbearable, and when we do, we make fools of ourselves.

Some Belarusian dissidents, however, do not have the luxury of taking this for granted. They are dissidents who have been forced into exile. They operate a Belarusian oppositional news website from their new living rooms in Lithuania, from the safety and security of the European Union. The website, called *Charter '97,* is illegal to access within the borders of Belarus. It suffers from near-constant cyber attacks. The year before I moved to Minsk, the website's founder, Aleh Byabenin, was found hanging from the rafters of his summer *dacha.* The authorities ruled it suicide.

Though I am an amateur—a foreigner, a fraud, and certainly not a dissident—the Belarusian opposition must agree with something I've written because they steal my words, translate them, and reprint them in their own underground corner of the internet. My essay appears in *Charter '97* without my permission. Twenty-first century *samizdat.*

Less than 24 hours after the dissidents repost my essay, I get a phone call from my boss at the university in Minsk. *You will probably need to leave the country,* she says, but what she means is that I am a snake in the grass. I am a traitor. I am a troublemaker. I have betrayed her, I have betrayed my students. She means that I have broken the first unspoken rule of places with dictators, which is that unless you want it to become as absolute as Ceaușescu's Romania, you cannot talk about it. Of course the dictator is everywhere—in every tree and limb—but you must not mention him. Pay no attention to the man hanging there.

Anyone who hears that, said Edgar, is bound to think you've lost your mind.

When I get off the phone, I am sick at how fixed and firm this rule feels, though still no one has ever said it to me. It is straightforward as sunshine, at once too big and too obvious to be treated with words. As a rule, only fools deal in poetry.

In 1979, many years before she writes her novel *The Land of Green Plums,* Herta Müller is dismissed from her job at a factory because she refuses to cooperate with the Romanian secret police. A man wearing a windbreaker visits her at work, says to her, *I know you better than you know tulips,* which are arranged neatly in a vase on her desk. He wants her to spy on people close to her. He calls it *collaborating*, which sounds like artists creating.

Müller tells the windbreaker man, *I don't have the character for this*, and so he smashes her tulip vase against the wall. She says that when it shattered it sounded like the air had teeth. In 2009 she is awarded the Nobel Prize for literature. In her acceptance speech, Müller acknowledges that what can't be said can still be written, that the subject of dictatorship is necessarily present because its characters are wholly robbed of the ability to take anything for granted. The dictator is always there, implied, while words spell out what the tongue cannot pronounce.

> The words in our mouths do as much damage as our feet on the grass. But so do our silences. Edgar was silent.

When Müller wins the Nobel Prize, Metropolitan Books in New York releases a striking English edition of *The Land of Green Plums*. The cover is green with orange accents and a clip-art statue of Lenin. His left arm is pointing straight ahead over the grassy hill, gesturing toward some future. In the writer's bio, it says that Müller lost her job as a teacher for not cooperating with the state, but this is a misprint, a small mistake. She wasn't a teacher; she was translating descriptions of hydraulic machines at a factory. Müller says the factory is where she first started writing, where she realized that language is hungry, that it begs to consume her experiences. The factory is where she first learned that language is wolfish.

Gluttony is a thing I, too, understand.

II. *Soviet Ukrainian Dissent: A Study of Political Alienation,* Jaroslaw Bilocerkowycz, 1988

For the first 23 years of my life, I do not open the book because it looks dull. The cover is communist red, the color of tomato paste, with plain white text and no pictures. As a child I couldn't pronounce two of the words in the title, which meant that it must be boring. Even though my father's name is on the front and my mother's on the inside—*To Sandra*—, and even though it follows me to every bookshelf in every apartment in every country I live, I do not open it until after I return from Belarus. By then I think I know what "dissent" and "alienation" mean.

Although in the mid-80s my mother is an actuary and not a political scientist, she helps with editing and research. She accompanies my father to New York City to interview Valentyn Moroz, a famous Soviet dissident and defector. My father's dissertation becomes a book and is published the same year I am born, *the best year of my life,* he says, which is three years before the dissolution of the USSR. My parents divorce when I am one year old, and my mother gives me all her copies of the red book. It is regimented that I should see my father for six weeks every year, and I am maybe fifteen when he starts asking, *Have you read my book yet?* I am a teenager, and though I am charmed by the fact that I can tell other people, *My father has published a real book!,* it still doesn't look very interesting. I tell him I have skimmed parts.

At 18 it is time to go to college, and I attend the university in Ohio where my father teaches. We begin having regular dinner dates and I realize I am learning about him for the first time. He tells me about his research trips to the USSR, about the feeling of having his book published, about interviewing Valentyn Moroz in his apartment. Moroz had just been released from a Soviet prison prior to his US defection. My father gets quiet when he tells me these things. I follow his lead. We inhabit a register below the

Someone is always hovering over Ukrainians, lest they become too interested in their own history.

ping of china and glassware. Despite what your instincts may tell you, a restaurant can be a good place to discuss sensitive matters. The house, the car, the office could be compromised. Email, too. If you are still free to move about the world, go out into it. A city park or a crowded, clanging restaurant—these offer something akin to privacy. A wide parking lot, perhaps. We pause mid-sentence when our waiter brings the check, a pair of mints.

At 18 I am reading Aristotle and Augustine and David Hume for class. I am reading Al-Bakri and Olaudah Equiano, Hannah Arendt and Elie Weisel. The world is expanding out in every direction. Despite what I had previously thought, it seems all the fields of earth—philosophy, religion, psychology, literature, politics—are actually *one*. My father tells me he has written about Ukraine for the newspaper and been interviewed for the television news. He tells me he has composed entries for real, hardcover encyclopedias. He is a source of Knowledge, my own father, a personal compendium! He wrote the encyclopedia entry for the NKVD! All the fields of earth are one, and my father is part of this grand historical context. You can find his book on Amazon.

I find my father's face on Wikipedia, too. He is protesting at Gasworks Park in Seattle with a group of Ukrainian immigrants in the '80s. They are worried about the proposed construction of a pipeline through Ukraine that they believe would make Europe dangerously dependent on Russian gas. My father holds a picket sign: Human Rights YES, Pipeline NO. He is part of some grand historical context. Maybe I am, too.

I finish college and move to Belarus. After I return home to the US, I am obsessed with ideas like dissent and alienation. I no longer take it for granted that writing is "safe" or "expressive" or even simply "art." After Belarus, I understand that writing has consequence and significance. It is hungry and dangerous. I decide this is a good time to sit down seriously with my father's book. I limit myself to small sections at a time, nervous about what I might find there.

I read about Iosyp Terelia, a longtime political and religious activist associated with the Ukrainian Catholic Church, which, for 45 years, is the largest underground church in the world. In 1983 he is sentenced to a one-year imprisonment for the crime of "parasitism." Since the Soviet Union is a workers' state, all able-bodied adults are expected to engage in "socially useful" work. If such adults refuse to do so for an extended period of time, they are considered parasitic. In order to avoid the charge, many dissidents and writers take up menial side work: street-sweeping, window-washing, making trinkets no one needs.

I read, too, about Valentyn Moroz. Back in the USSR he survived a prison-knifing and a 145-day hunger strike. I imagine my mother and father in Moroz's New York apartment, drinking tea with lemon, while he explained the mechanics of force-feeding. Prison guards strap you down to a table and shove a tube up your nose. Obviously, they have to break the cartilage. The tube is snaked into your throat, and though you would very much like to scream, the thing that comes out is soundless.

Moroz is first arrested in 1965 for possession of *samizdat* written by someone else, says it surprised him because the document wasn't even explicitly oppositional. He gets arrested again five years later, charged with "anti-Soviet agitation and propaganda" for publishing a series of three essays that circulate underground. In the essays, Moroz discusses the culture of fear, calling it a "giant refrigerator for human minds," brains that can no longer think or create independently from the Soviet state. He laments what he sees as calculated homogenizing, which he connects to the destruction of Ukrainian art by the Soviets.

A significant share of dissidents were literati.

But not just Ukrainian art. He cites suspicious fires that have occurred in major libraries across the USSR—in Kyiv, Tartu, Ashkhabad, Samarkand. How the casualties of these accidental fires were mostly ancient texts in the local native languages and how isn't it strange that no treasured libraries in Russia have ever burned?

I read about surveillance. How it takes a psychological and emotional toll, particularly when a dissident knows or suspects they have been bugged. I read about how nine KGB officers searched Oksana Meshko's apartment for 19 hours straight, and she wasn't even the main subject of the investigation. I read about Vera Lisova, the wife of a prominent dissident, who suffered a heart attack after a grueling KGB interrogation. As I read these pages to myself, the voice in my head quiets. The walls move a little closer.

Petro Grigorenko, for example, estimates that the regime used 23 security personnel in three shifts to monitor and keep him under surveillance over a four-year period at a cost of 200,000 rubles.

Sometimes, if you're under surveillance, the people watching will leave a sign. They will scatter the papers on your desk. Situate a half-drunk cup of tea. Dresser drawers flung open. Sometimes, they want you to know about them. Once you spy a clump of blonde hair in the sink, everything is different for you. Grass will begin to grow where your brain once was. A smell of almonds. Did I see that car earlier? Right turn, right turn, right turn . . . Work, grocery store, home. Work, grocery store, home. Do not deviate from this pattern. Give them no reason to be suspicious. Bore them. You have a cold. Do not talk about illegally downloading mp3s. Do not talk about fudging on your taxes or smoking a joint. Avoid these activities altogether. And if you can help it, do not own a cell phone. If you must, then vagueness is a virtue. You may even grow to like it, this feeling of perpetual company.

I hold my father's book. The cover is the color of heat, of something scorching. The walls closer than before.

I read about Volodymyr Ivasyuk, a young Ukrainian composer. He is famous for composing popular songs in the Ukrainian language. They are love songs, mostly. But when the Soviet authorities ask him to compose something in Russian, trouble begins. He refuses their request. Cue the nail clippers. Cue the pounding head cold. In springtime the poet is found hanging from a tree in the forest outside Lviv. Ivasyuk was last seen alive in KGB custody, but the authorities rule his death a suicide.

Please don't go searching
For the red bloom this evening.

My face is blushing. I am embarrassed by how I love these awful stories and what they teach me about my father, his voice lowered in the back rooms of restaurants, his suspicions, his picket sign. The red book is 242 pages of suffering, and it cannot be separated from our family. I gorge myself on the stories, as I imagine my father had once done himself. My father wrote the encyclopedia entry for the NKVD! My father, a personal compendium.

Sometimes when I am in a new city or on a strange campus, I go to the library to see if they have the red book. Not necessarily to read it or check it out, just to hold it. I don't know why I do this. I already own multiple copies. My father never remarried, has only a few close friends, and no other children besides me. Each time a relative dies—from old age, suicide, disease—their copy of the red book is given to me. It is usually inscribed with their names in ballpoint pen, a regular greeting, a little book of the dead spelled out in hieroglyphs. Ravenous, I swallow them whole.

This is my inheritance.

III. *The Captive Mind*, Czesław Miłosz, 1953

My boss breathes heavily into the phone. *You will probably need to leave the country,* she says, but what she means is that I am a snake in the grass. I am a traitor. I am a troublemaker.

They suspend me from my job at the university, and I am told to wait for further instructions. I am too afraid to leave my apartment. I have made a huge mistake, publishing this stupid essay. I am from the land of brown grass and ponderosa pines, and I don't know the danger of unripe fruit because all I've ever had are chokecherries, which are small and desperate and not like real fruit at all. This *dictator* word was only ever abstract, imported through books and movies, Orwell, Huxley, Rand. I am taken by old tropes, and I am naïve. When my co-workers at the state university pointed to the ceiling and rolled their eyes, I figured this meant they were tired of the dictator. I figured this meant they would agree with me.

Officially, contradictions do not exist in the minds of the citizens in the people's democracies.

For maybe a week after the phone call from my boss, I sleep on the couch and do not leave the apartment. I don't know why, but I am afraid of my bedroom. On the couch I have dreams about pulling tap wires out of the green wallpaper. They run like streams up to the ceiling. I am haunted there, but certain that if I leave the living room, men in dark jackets will be waiting with nail clippers. They will descend from the sky the way crows do on a picnic. They will catch me and hold me under bare light bulbs. There will be clippers where bird talons should be, a strong smell of almonds. I have mowed the grass too short this time, a real inconvenience. I will have to write my mother and tell her about my cold, the pounding head cold, the one living inside me like a parasite. She will be so disappointed I have gone and gotten myself sick.

Hi Mom,,,,,,,,,,,

During this week on the couch, I am groping for anything to explain my predicament. My boss at the university used to tell me about how difficult the government made her life, how they were always interfering and implementing silly laws, how pitiable her salary was. Why, then, is she so angry with me? I have only pointed toward the dictator.

On the couch, I read about Ketman in Miłosz's *The Captive Mind* and think maybe I've found an answer. Ketman is a Persian concept used to describe the state of mind of a person who chooses to believe one thing, while practicing or vocalizing another. It is, you could say, an intentional or protective form of cognitive dissonance. For Miłosz, writing in Communist Poland, Ketman is a professional survival tool. It is paying lip service to the oppressive regime while concealing one's true opposition. But Ketman involves more than mere silence; it is an active façade, a complex psychological game of appearances. Ketman is acting, but instead of a theater stage it is done on the street corner, at the chalkboard, in the bedroom.

My presence in the university department upset the standard rules of the game. My co-workers wanted me, the American, to understand that *they* understood their own government to be an undemocratic nuisance. But just because they were comfortable disparaging the dictator around me, does not mean I was in a position to disparage him myself. Miłosz says these contradictions pose a special problem for a country's intellectuals.

> A writer who has not consecrated a single work to outstanding Russian figures or to Russian life . . . cannot consider himself entirely safe.

I am camped in the living room, waiting for the hulking men who will interrogate me into a heart attack. I tell one local friend how frightened I am about being sent to a Belarusian prison. *When Victor went to prison after the election protests we all sewed him socks and mittens,* she says. *I sewed his name onto the mittens. It was really very sweet.* She smiles and laughs a little, as if we were discussing something average. A baby shower, perhaps.

The hulking men never show up. I hear nothing at all for two weeks and am uninvolved in my own fate. Then, I receive another phone call. I am informed that "perhaps" if I write something "more positive" we might be able to negotiate. It is a cryptic suggestion. I don't understand how writing a follow-up essay would help, unless, of course, I were to say that I didn't mean any of it in the first place. I explain that I cannot lie, but that I do really want a second chance to teach my courses. I agree to try writing something more . . . positive.

I open a blank Word document. I am trembling like an old tram. But as I move through sentences, I start to feel grateful. I am glad to be writing about Belarusian food and hospitality and my dear friends here, the people who seemed shocked at my earlier indiscretion. *Why didn't you write about my mother's cookies?* a friend had asked after reading the essay on *Charter '97.* I didn't have a good answer. Her mother makes amazing sugar cookies, but I had written instead about some cookies, purchased at Minsk's fancy central grocery store, that were crawling with worms. I guess I am drawn to rot. And, if I'm honest, I had not intended for Belarusians to read the essay at all. The dialogue was stilted from the start.

I contact the editor of the US-based travel website. He is confused about why I would need to publish a "positive" follow-up, which is exactly what Miłosz said would happen, for those in the West do not need Ketman. The editor is American. I am also American, I explain to him, and I have

> What can be said openly is often much less interesting than the emotional magic of defending one's private sanctuary.

only just now begun to understand how frightening it is to find a pair of nail clippers on the kitchen counter, not at all where you left them. I have only just now begun to feel the mucous build-up in my throat, signs of an awful, inevitable head cold. I have only just now taken up acting.

In fact, I do not say any of this to the American editor, but I think you understand.

IV. *Depeche Mode,* Serhiy Zhadan, 2004

When I purchase the book in spring 2014, I am living in western Ukraine, not far from where my father's father and my father's mother grew up. Although Serhiy Zhadan is one of Ukraine's most famous living writers, this is, at the time, his only novel I can find in English translation.

Zhadan's characters reside in Kharkiv, an eastern Ukrainian city 1,000 km away from where I am living. Zhadan is a poet turned prose writer, and you can tell; his sentences are long and winding, wild but rhythmic in a way that makes sense to some people, like jazz. In *Depeche Mode* it is the early 90s, and one-sixth of Earth's land surface is spinning off from the Soviet Union. Ukraine is in chaos. A swirling cast of young characters deal with the fallout: The communist headquarters is now an advertising agency. Depeche Mode is no longer on bootlegged tapes, but on the radio. American preachers wearing Rolex watches sermonize in city squares to thousands, but even the hired translator doesn't speak English. Fatherless boys invest in vodka smuggled cheaply over the Russian border. The economy has tanked, and nihilists drink the day away on trolley buses. Everything is absurd.

The English translation has enough misprints to notice, but I keep reading anyways because Zhadan's reputation is illustrious. I also keep reading because it feels personal: in 2014 I

am teaching at a university in Lviv, Ukraine, and Zhadan's son
is one of my students. He is 17 and nervous. His hands shake
when he passes his homework to me. He smells like cigarettes,
wears mostly black, and once
acts as Tim Burton for a celebrity speech assignment. He gives
a brilliant performance. I want
to ask Zhadan's son which of
his father's books he most rec-
ommends, but I don't want to
embarrass him. I hear from another student that he says he
hasn't read any of them.

> She's sitting there, probably,
> on the balcony with her arms
> around the copper bust of
> Molotov who for some reason
> resembles her dad the gen-
> eral. Why can't she sit like
> that with her dad?

I read *Depeche Mode* in the months when Lenin statues are
falling across Ukraine. Lenin, the first great defender of the so-
cialist fatherland, has fire at his feet and ropes around his neck
all over the country. The major Lenin statue in downtown Kyiv
is toppled in December 2013 during the second week of anti-
government protests that will eventually run the pro-Kremlin
president, Viktor Yanukovych, out of office and over the Russian border.

Like his characters, Serhiy Zhadan is from Kharkiv, the
second largest Ukrainian city, home to mostly Russian speakers. Zhadan was born speaking Russian, too, but now writes in
Ukrainian. He is an activist, though his politics are neither un-
critically pro-Western nor anti-Russian. I hear him give a talk
in February, just days before the final firestorm of the revolution. *Yanukovych has long lost legitimacy,* he says. *When the EU
deals with Yanukovych, they need to understand that they are
dealing with a dictator.* He signs my copy of his book with long,
upright letters in blue ink: ЖАДАН.

Some political scientists will likely disagree with the "dictator" label, though Yanukovych isn't democratic, to be sure. He
famously falsifies an election in 2004, causes Ukraine to lose 40

points on the Press Freedom Index, throws his political opponents in prison, and uses his state security agents liberally. But it is perhaps more accurate to call him a simple crook. Conservative estimates place his stolen wealth at 24 billion dollars. His is a kleptocracy, and when the regime is finally ousted, the people will storm his presidential estate and eventually convert it into a public park. I, too, will peer into the windows of his newly built mansion at Mezhyhirya and see $64,000 Lebanese wooden doors under light refracted from $100,000 crystal chandeliers. On the marble table I imagine the ghost of recent food. Meat. Champagne. Cookies. Golden Fabergé eggs.

When the revolution starts there are no guarantees that it will succeed, and this is the biggest risk. My university is outspoken and active, encouraging its students to skip class in order to go protest. The administration organizes buses to Kyiv, and though the air is electric with talk of change, the old order is still intact.

One day in December, officers from the state security service (SBU, a new acronym for an old thing—KGB) visit the dean of the school, talk to him in his office, which is right across the hall from mine. The SBU men ask for names of students participating in the demonstrations. They want to see attendance rosters. The dean refuses, saying *our student records are private,* and the SBU officers tell him that criminal cases are being opened against them. I imagine the men smashing a vase of tulips before exiting, though I'm certain this did not actually happen. I was across the hall, I would have heard it, the sound of teeth. My students confirm the intimidation: they receive phone calls interrogating their activities, warning them about being vocal online. I am amazed how none of them seem deterred by this.

The situation escalates in mid-January when Yanukovych rams a series of anti-protest laws through parliament. On paper, Ukraine looks like a dictatorship, but in the streets people dissent. These are the weeks of men in Audis delivering bottles, rags, and petrol to the front line. From February 18th to 22nd over a hundred people—mostly protestors, some police officers—die on Maidan from sniper fire, and by the 23rd Yanukovych has fled the country

> Comrade! Make a Molotov cocktail! A Molotov cocktail is not a real cocktail; it is an explosive mixture. The enemy cannot put this flame out with water.

in his helicopter. During these five days alone, 219 Lenin statues are reportedly toppled throughout Ukraine. It is called Leninopad, a Leninfall, a waterfall.

Most mayors and governors of the eastern regions flee, too, and in the power vacuum, cities like Kharkiv turn especially violent. Clashes between pro-Westerners and pro-Russians are like small microcosms of the whole country and when strange troops with Russian accents are spotted in Crimea, the question of "West" or "East" becomes more literal than theoretical. In early March Zhadan is acting as an organizer for an ongoing pro-Ukrainian rally in Kharkiv when counter-protestors storm their building. "Cuts on the head, eyebrow dissected, concussion, broken nose suspected," he writes on his Facebook page. He says when the men are beating him, they order him to kneel and kiss the Russian flag. Zhadan tells them to go fuck themselves.

> This is the greatest secret of civilization. Society devours itself.

As Russia annexes Crimea and sends tanks over the border into the Donbass, the revolution becomes a war and one of my students says in class that *this is like 400 years of history happening in four months,* and another student says in another class that *I don't think those old people really miss the USSR—they just miss their youth,* and I am exhausted by these expanses of time, our grand historical context.

Three months after Zhadan is sent to the hospital, I visit a prison in Lviv. It is no longer a functioning prison, but a small museum, a memorial to the victims of communist oppression. There, I attend a talk given by Valentyn Moroz, who has just released a new history book. The building's exterior is modest (I accidentally pass it on the street), though the place is intimately tied to the dramatic history Moroz writes about. The prison served as the KGB's regional interrogation and detention center until 1991 and now displays the delicate and aging relics of its dissident inmates: seized *samizdat,* eyeglasses, rosaries made of tiny balls of bread, embroidery done with fish bones for needles.

There are 10 of us, maybe 15, who show up to hear Moroz speak. Most are older men, his contemporaries. The skin on Moroz's face is gray like frost and sagging. He talks slowly, the cadence of his 78-year-old voice echoing the horrible things he's seen—or, at least in my imagination it does this. When he is asked about the ongoing Russian invasion, he responds matter-of-factly, *Russia again wants to drive Ukraine back into its cell. But that is no longer possible.* He even smiles, as if this is obvious. The narrow prison room has been arranged with a few folding chairs, but is otherwise just concrete and cold, the walls pea green, a bare light bulb above Moroz's head. It looks like an interrogation room.

Back home in the US, I watch the news stream from a small computer screen, now seven hours behind. The destruction of the Donetsk airport, Malaysia Flight 17, the capture of Debaltseve, cluster bombs, sanctions, elections. History is on fast forward, or maybe on replay. The new Ukrainian government blames Russia for the civilian deaths, and in response the Russian authorities blame Ukraine. The country is a giant stage for all manner of *provokatsiya,* that is, provocation. A pro-Russian might enact violence in the disguise of a pro-Ukrainian, and vice versa. *Provokatsiya.* Several Ukrainian Jewish rabbis accuse Kremlin operatives of anti-Semitic vandalism, calling it a ploy by Moscow to buttress its own propaganda campaign against Ukrainians. *Provokatsiya*. The absurd, it seems, is not just a literary notion. It is a political strategy.

I follow Serhiy Zhadan on Facebook. It is Ukrainian Christmas, January 7th, 2015, when he posts a short verse, the absurd summed up:

Freedom usually lies in the fact
of voluntarily returning to prison.

V. *The Master and Margarita,* Mikhail Bulgakov, 1966

No one sews socks for me, because I do not go to prison. I am not deported. I am not even fired from my job. I cannot explain why this is the case, but it is. The American editor agrees to publish my "positive" follow-up, and my boss invites me back to work. I did not retract the original essay, but confessed that perhaps I was guilty of pointing too hard in one direction. Perhaps my vision was a wolfish, narrow one.

For reasons I am never told and do not understand, I am allowed to return to my students. I apologize to them, and I mean it, though I am not sure if I am sorry for pointing too hard—for trimming the grass too short— or simply for being a fool. My students are

—Where is your permanent residence?
—I have none, I travel from town to town.

not satisfied with my brief, embarrassed explanation, and so they corner me after class. Theirs is my only interrogation.

What happened to you?
Where have you been?
We were worried about you.
We missed you.

I tell them everything is fine, I'm fine. I am still too nervous to admit otherwise. One of my students, a young woman with dyed blonde hair and hipster glasses, says, *We know you got in trouble, even though you didn't do anything.* She has a mustache tattooed on her pointer finger, which must be useful for mocking the dictator, who has one growing on his face. I want to correct this student and say that I did, in fact, do something, that I made the mistake of speaking about unspeakable things, and even though nobody told me the rules, I could have probably guessed them. I really should have known better. But before I can say this, another student stops me. He has worked very hard this year to get rid of his Russian accent, and when this student speaks, it is difficult to place him. *It's silly,* he says, with absolutely no emotion, *but that's how things work in this country.*

When I finally return to my own bed, I read Bulgakov before falling asleep. I am just now getting acquainted with the absurd, and for some inexplicable reason I am drawn to Annushka, a woman who spills sunflower oil on the tram rails. (Is it because my grandmother gave me that nickname, *sonyash-nyk,* sunflower?) At the novel's start, a foreign professor who is really the devil in disguise visits Moscow. He informs Berlioz, chairman of the Moscow literary club, that something awful is due to happen: Berlioz will not make it to tonight's meeting because of decapitation. Annushka has already bought the oil. She has already spilled it on the tracks. His fate is sealed. Berlioz brushes off the grim prediction by this mysterious professor, though later, in another part of the city, the tram barrels as if from a gun and Berlioz moves behind a turnstile toward safety. But! He slips on a bit of oil. The old tram shakes on its way by, and Berlioz's severed head ricochets off the cobblestones.

—Who are you by blood?
—I don't know exactly.

I consider Berlioz's false sense of security again a few weeks later, when I am invited to give a guest lecture to a class of students from a different department of the university. I take a *marshrutka* minibus to the outskirts of Minsk and a few friendly passengers help me find the correct classroom building. Here, we are past the city's ring road, and the air feels lighter, spread thin. I cannot believe my good luck, how I have avoided prison and deportation. How I get to watch the trees change green in this strange dictatorship.

A co-worker meets me at the entrance to the building. He walks me through a set of metal turnstiles with green lights and waves to the uniformed woman sitting nearby. She nods. Her hair is set with heaps of hairspray. *They installed these this year,* my co-worker says, gesturing to the turnstiles. *Just another silly thing.*

Why's that? I ask.

Well, it's sort of funny actually, he explains. *There was a government mandate which said the university must install them, for control, but they found when the morning rush happens there's a huge line of students and professors that all end up late for class. Three of these—what do you call them?*

Turnstiles, I say.

Three turnstiles can't handle hundreds of people. So now they just leave them on green all day and don't bother checking ID cards. They only turn them on to red when a Ministry member comes for inspection.

What about random checks? I ask.

We don't have any. Everything has to be mandated first. And besides, he gives a half-smile, *no one really wants to catch anyone doing something wrong.*

I will never forget the look on his face when he said this. There was a particular kindness in his half-smile, as if he were delivering an answer to a soundless question. And like most things under the dictator, it was an answer delivered in code. Admittedly, I am afraid to set even this small story in ink. I am afraid I may still be a troublemaker. Will they know the turnstile woman by her hairspray? Will they care?

Bulgakov was terrified, too. He burned an early copy of *The Master and Margarita,* understanding that he would be a target of the NKVD if it were leaked. But the text and its characters haunted him. They would not leave him alone. Over several years Bulgakov rewrote the manuscript, dictating some portions to his wife, though it would not be published in full until long after his death. For a while in the late 1960s, the unedited version circled underground as *samizdat.*

—Can you read and write?
—Yes.

In the novel, the character of the Master writes a book himself, about Pontius Pilate interrogating Christ. When the foreign professor asks to see his book, the Master admits that he burned it in the stove. *Forgive me,* the professor responds, *but I don't believe you. That cannot be, manuscripts don't burn.* Right then, in the room where they are chatting, the cat jumps off a chair and the pages of the Master's manuscript appear in its place. It has reappeared out of nowhere. The text will not go away, which is something I am only just now coming to understand.

It has been over seven years since I published the first little essay, those vignettes I thought were clever hieroglyphs. *Charter '97* refused to take down the essay, and so I still receive the occasional message from a stranger. They have read my words, and they are angry. Or, they have read my words, and they relate. Or, they have read my words and do not appreciate the discussion of wormy cookies because our cookies are really very tasty, and this was a fluke, and cookies don't mean anything anyways, you silly girl. It does not matter which. The point is that language is hungry, and once it has consumed the experience you can never take it back. Manuscripts don't burn. Perhaps the code of this text is getting away from me now, for I am not meant to sound like the hero. I am not Bulgakov. I am not Christ. I am not even poor Berlioz who mistook the turnstiles for safety. No, I am more like Annushka, not an important character, just a regular woman. An average sort of troublemaker, reckless with the lawnmower. I have only spilt a little oil, which cannot be easily cleaned up.

THE VILLAGE (INTERLUDE)

After the prison, I visit the village. A friend of a friend drives us there. He has two small flags suctioned to his dashboard, one Ukrainian and one European Union. The road into the village is old stones, and as we drive our tires cause rocks to ricochet. The way is lined with wooden telephone poles. Some of them are topped with plump stork nests, like grassy lollipops stuck into the mouth of the sky. This is where Busia grew up and where she once filled jars of soil to smuggle back to America.

When we arrive, Busia's cousin Marina is out back with the chickens. She did not know we were coming. There are red and blue bruises around her mouth. She fell down last week, but don't worry, relax, it looks worse than it feels, everything is alright. Marina nods when I explain how we are related. She vaguely recalls we have met before.

The yard is teeming. Bird feathers, blossoms, cabbage, carrots, onion shoots. There is a field of screaming yellow rapeseed behind the house. A cat wanders about, a goat in the yard next door. Rainbows, jewel tones, floral embroidery on every wall. Marina didn't know we were coming and insists on getting dressed up for the occasion. She finds her good headscarf in the bedroom and ties it beneath her bruised chin. We smile at how our scarves match. On the kitchen table is a mailer from the Party of Regions, the political party of the newly ex-president, the one who just absconded in his helicopter to Russia. STABIL-ITY AND PROSPERITY. NEUTRAL FOREIGN POLICY. OPEN-NESS AND NEIGHBORLINESS. I wonder if Paul Manafort helped write these trinkets, which remind me of Lukashenko's insistence that stability is the great Belarusian "brand." Do people believe it? When you worry about waking up in new empires, does stability become the highest possible good? I am told there is a local woman here who supports the Party of Regions. She helps elderly villagers vote by pointing to which box they should check on the ballot. Marina has very bad eyes, and I wonder if the woman has helped her, too.

Beside the mailer, Marina doodled roses on a list of monthly bills to be paid. I admire the detail of her thorns. I leave a box of cherry cordials there on the table. They are from the chocolate factory owned by the new president, the one who took over after the revolution. Sitting here, you would never know the country is at war with its neighbor. Marina does not own a television, so she will hear news of peace treaties, signed and broken, on the radio. History will be presented in tidy segments bookended by English pop songs.

We decide to go for a walk because Marina does not own a car. Her nephew, Yarosh, who also lives in the village, owns only a tractor and a bicycle. Neither of them has ever left the village. They do not have refrigerators or indoor plumbing, but on a day as clear blue as this one, I think I might enjoy relieving myself in the field.

Marina talks about change. She points to where my grandmother's house used to be. The village once had rolling hills and dense tree groves, but the Soviets flattened all that. The imaginary house she points to is where my great-grandfather—the

village mayor, the patriot, the reluctant dissenter, the myth—
also lived. Knock, knock. Marina's mother went looking for
him after his arrest. She traveled to the prison in the nearest
town, and that was the last anyone saw him.

I ask if Marina wants to stroll to the cemetery with me and
she says, *I would go to America with you if you asked,* and we
both laugh because it sounds silly, which is sad. I am sad because of how callous it is, all this leaving and returning and
leaving again, the loops that history makes. I imagine myself as
a voice in the wilderness, when in fact maybe I am part of the
problem. Maybe I am another cog in the cyclic machine of oppression, moving about with foolish intentions, writing things
no one needs. Lines of tin sheep. Wooden watermelon poems.

We pause for a moment in the chicken yard. Marina is lock-
ing the house door behind us with a heavy padlock, which
seems odd to me, though I don't mention it. OPENNESS AND
NEIGHBORLINESS. The village is so small and so rural. I'm not
sure what there is to steal. A teakettle?

As we walk arm-in-arm through the light blue headstones,
we talk about the war. The grass is dandelion-speckled and tall,
the apple branches above us drooping with white flowers, soon-
to-be fruit. I see dirt in each crease of Marina's face and hands,
and all of this makes me nostalgic, makes me read meaning
into each limb and blossom. The village graveyard's shade of
eggshell blue has become a symbol. Whenever I see it in the
world, I see death. *What does Putin want with us anyways?* Marina asks, sheepish and smiling, almost self-deprecating in her
humility. A few yards away the cemetery caretaker overhears
her question and stops working. He leans against a shovel and
shakes his head. The three of us marvel in silence. Maybe, *What
do they want with us?* is the same question I am trying to answer, only by way of a hundred confused and lyrical diversions,
pages and pages of trinkets. Maybe, what can't be said still begs
to be written.

White storks are nesting above us on a wooden telephone pole. They clatter their bills, while Marina, the graveyard man, and I stand quietly. We are fumbling for words that could pass for an answer. We don't find any.

ENCYCLOPEDIA OF EARTHLY THINGS

The word encyclopedia comes from the Koine Greek . . .

from *enkyklios,* meaning "circular, recurrent, revolving"

and *paideia,* meaning "education, rearing of a child."

—Wikipedia.org

A STORK

It watches our black earth from its nest on a telephone pole. Electricity moves through it. It is white. Its only sound is bill-clattering, like a machine gun firing rounds. There is one assigned to every peasant family. It works for the NKVD.

Commonly found in western Ukraine, the land of Bandera, where there is a lot of earth to watch. It watches our peasant family and reports back to headquarters. It keeps tabs on our great uncles and their fathers. It knows when to swoop in for the arrest. We are taken to prison in the next town over. Some of us survive prison. Some of us don't. Its only sound is bill-clattering. It brings endings.

It brings beginnings. We arrive in its beak, dangling over the wheat. We arrive in its beak, wrapped in a *rushnyk* of linen, red flowers embroidered to the edges. The red flowers are a map of life. We are baptized and buried with them. We arrive in its beak, wailing our earliest songs. Upon landing, we already know how to mourn.

POPPY

Suggests sleep. Petals of red paper, easily lost. Suggests virginity. The seeds are like fish eggs. Ask for caviar by saying *ikra*; ask for poppy seeds in your loaf by saying *z makom*. It paints itself in a line through the wheat fields. A streak of blood is too easy, but that's why the government made it a symbol. It's supposed to help people like our grandmothers never forget the war, like *I not remember*. How could they? The most precious things are buried inside.

HERRING (ANIMAL)

Best pickled. Best dead. It smells like rotting, like that stack of bodies left out in the sun the next town over. I don't know what it looks like living.

HERRING (HUMAN)

It is the name for a traditional haircut in which a long cord sprouts from the top of an otherwise closely shaven head. Alternate name: *khokhol*. It is a style most often associated with the *kobzari,* a class of blind, roving bards who play stringed instruments and sing in the Ukrainian language. Their songs are secretly poems.

In 1930 the Soviets host an ethnographic conference in Kharkiv and invite *kobzari* from every region. Hundreds attend. The idea is to integrate regional folk musicians into the project of socialism. After the first day, organizers pack the honored *kobzari* guests onto train cars and drive them outside the city to a dark part of the forest. Trenches have already been dug. They line up the blind bards and open fire. Records of this execution have never been found, but it is a true story we often tell.

If a tree without papers falls in the forest, does it make a sound?

BLACK SOIL

It is *chornozem*. It is burnt. It has all the acids good for growing. It is primarily composed of dead things. It is like land after a fire, a very fertile situation. It surrounds our cousin's house and the houses of her neighbors. When we return to the village, and stand in the place where our own house once stood, we will scoop the ground into jars and bring it home. Better we take it, than someone else. Back in Chicagoland, our grandmothers hide the jars on the top shelves of their closets.

As Europe's breadbasket, we are world famous for it. Sometimes truckloads are stolen out from under us. There is a black market for *chornozem*. In a nutshell, we are fighting over dead cells.

COAL

It is the other black earth. It is a monster. We throw down good men and it swallows. It coats the floors of mafia caves in the Donbass. The Donbass is the Dontes Basin, a portmanteau, a region in the East famous for this stuff. The mafia caves are illegal, no regulations, no safety checks. Today there is also a war in the Donbass. The Donbass swallows. We are throwing all our good men down there now.

It is forever night. The miner ties a light to his head. The only sound is bill-clattering, the rounds of his jackhammer. The country runs on this noise. He emerges from the mafia caves with a dim, leaden face. He looks in mirrors and does not see himself. He is handed an envelope of Monopoly money, rainbow banknotes. The watercolor faces of dead poets stare back at him. The country runs on these. It is a monster.

THE CORNER of a TABLE

It is sharp like a cliff-face. If you're single and hope to marry, do not sit here.

A WILD BOAR

It is a mountain dinosaur left over. Its back is a set of tectonic plates, rising. We take its shanks. We take its *salo*. Last year's pig, this year's pig, next year's and the one after that. Food is anything that helps you carry on.

It roams the continent. In 1986, after the reactor blows up, scientists find it in Germany, its gut lined with caesium-137. Where it used to live, there aren't any people left. Only a forest of fancy truffles, rare delicacies, still and untouched. We would take those, too, but, you know.

A WINDOW

Square-shaped. Landing pad for ladybugs. Do not throw a potato out of it. At nighttime it becomes a mirror.

THE OSTRICHES

They are women in the shape of birds. They are birds passing for women. Viktor Y., the ex-president, isn't sure where they came from. After he absconds in his helicopter, revolutionaries find a flock hanging about the presidential sauna, dangling their legs over ledges, lazily painting their nails. The revolutionaries cry *Korruptsiya! Corruption!* Later, when a journalist asks how he paid for the private zoo, the ex-president's face gets shiny. *I supported the ostriches*, he says, *what's wrong with that?* They are not native, so I don't have much else to say.

AN ONION

It is a ghost vegetable, which means it is everywhere and nowhere, forever and ever. Its beige papers blow across the counter when we open the back door. They collect like dead leaves between the stove and refrigerator, our own little archive. We try not to look down there.

A BIRCH

It is straight. It is white. Can be used to sweep for demons. *Samizdat* is written into its soft bark. Dostoevsky calls it *the strength of the Russian land.* Other uses: Carve an instrument. Drink its sap. Beat a naughty child (twigs intact). Mix its leaves in hot water to treat an upset stomach.

One time, our great-uncle is starving. He is a starving boy. Starving. Everyone is starving. His neighbor chases him because he is starving, too. Our great-uncle is light enough to climb it. It bows to the East, but only slightly. The neighbor is too heavy. He paws at the bark below, howling, *yak volk,* hungry as a wolf.

Up there, the starving boy is eye-to-eye with the stork.

A WHISTLE

It belongs on the street. It belongs in the Park of Culture and Recreation. It belongs in the market. It belongs in between puffs of a cigarette. It does not belong inside your house, unless you intend to call the devil. The devil is from Donbass. He dresses like a professor, and it won't take him long to get here.

A MOUFLON

It is wild. It is tri-colored. It used to live in Crimea. Now, we're not sure where that is. Its horns twist round and round. Its horns are history.

AMBER

It comes from birch resin. It comes from muddy mafia bogs. It traps kindly water bugs. It is a sunflower field you can hold in your hand, or tie around your neck. The men are called *starateli,* prospectors. They slash and burn; they wade; they fish with nets. They can't eat it, but the mafia boss gives them rainbow-stained notes per kilo collected. They can't eat those either.

KYIV, UKRAINE

It is the center of old empires and new. It is the center of revolution. It is sliced in two by a groaning river, knifed by a green ravine, topped with a rainbow. It is the seventh largest city in Europe. Coordinates: 50.4501° N, 30.5234° E.

If you're wondering why Y and not E, it's because one is the Ukrainian transliteration and the other is Russian. If you're wondering why not *the* Ukraine, it's because we don't need the article. We are perfectly fine on our own.

ICON of ST. VOLODYMYR the GREAT

It is gold-leafed. It shimmers. It hangs in the corner. His face is the one that converted the country. There's a halo about his head. His halo is made from the way sunlight reflects on water.

TCDD DIOXIN

It is odorless. It is colorless. It is burnt. It is primarily composed of dead things. It is untraceable in soup.

Viktor Y. (the other ex-president) calls it poison. In the election season of 2004, Viktor Y. (the other ex-president) is running against Viktor Y. (the absconder). One night during the campaign, he is eating with colleagues. He emerges from the mafia dinner with a dim, leaden face. He looks in mirrors and does not see himself. His skin is boiling; bloating; pockmarked. His skin is the burnt earth, secrets gathered into molehills. They mushroom up and out toward the light. His skin pulls the poison away from vital organs. Politicians are rich enough to roam the continent, so in Austria scientists try to save him. They call it poison, too. They explain the issue of fat solubility: *A cream soup, for example.*

A GOLDEN BEET

The sun is too easy, but what else is there to say? The earth's most precious thing hovers above.

DNIPRO RIVER

It comes from Russian turf swamps. It is wide as 10 villages. It severs the land. It washes down chemicals like tablets. It chokes on incriminating documents. It hums. The dead poets call it *roaring* and *groaning.* As if it were a lion, which is not native. As if it were a starving man, which is.

A DOLPHIN

It rings the peninsula, which is an exact place we can no longer locate exactly. Its snout clatters like a jackhammer, clicks like bullet shells. It is a Black Sea defense strategy. We train it for war. We engage it in NATO exercises. We tie a harpoon to its head, claim it for whichever empire is winning. It is useful for disorienting enemy sonar. The enemy is a moving target.

Did you know Sevastopol is one of only two military dolphin training facilities in the world? San Diego is the other.

A SPOON

It is whittled from a tree with white bark. It is a boat. It is a soup grotto. If it falls to the floor, expect a female visitor. We have a particular devotion to Our Lady.

A SUNFLOWER FIELD

It is a graveyard. It is a cemetery for Boeing plane parts. It is a Park of Remembrance for old tray tables, airline seats, oxygen masks, No Smoking signs in another language, steel wings, scorched safety cards. It is the opposite of a factory.

It is a burial ground for continental things: Dutch clogs, Winnie the Poohs, Cadbury chocolate. And continental bodies. The bodies are growing. They are planted in black soil, ears among the onions. They are organic matter, stretching to live. They are arms, legs, torsos, trying to reach the sky. They still have a long way to go.

ANOTHER SUNFLOWER FIELD

is just that.

A EUROPEAN BISON

It was shot years ago. If you're lucky enough to see it now, know that it comes from only one family, which comes from a zoo. I heard the Germans were particularly bad poachers during the war. They left us with just nine beasts. Really, this should surprise no one.

The Americans have their own version, with more ribs and less hair. At one point, the Americans had killed all but 100 beasts. Really, this should surprise no one.

A MARSHRUTKA

It is painted like the sun. It is a taxi that runs on a set route. It is a taxi on loop. After everything collapsed in the '90s, you had the Marshrutka Boom. This is how people traveled home. It is a chugging sun that runs around like history.

Inside we offer rainbow notes for a ride. Everyone is here. Everyone with their babies and their bouquets and their best-dead herring. Jesus and Volodymyr are here, too. They swing from the mirror above the driver's head, icon tassels dangling against the wheat field. The woman beside me coughs; an apple rolls out of my bag and onto the floor. It's a funny thing, this free market.

A MUSHROOM

It is fungal. It is a vacuum. It sucks through white threads spread in wide swaths below the soil. Its threads form blankets. There is a whole layer of earth made of white blankets. In fact, the world's largest organism is a fungal blanket underneath America.

It sucks caesium-137 through its threads. Put it in broth with a silver spoon and an onion to check. If it darkens, don't eat. Slice it and squeeze its milky liquid onto salt. If the salt yellows, don't eat.

Men do these checks and then load it on trucks. They send it across the continent where it is met by border control guards.

The continental guards don't appreciate how it glows. But we are world famous for that light.

A RAINBOW

The color of money. The color of repast eggs. If you stick your tongue out, it will dry up. Makes a full circle. From where we stand on earth, we just can't tell.

THE STEPPE

It is populated by soil-boring rodents. The dirt here is chestnut colored. The grass here spikes like feathers, falls like braids. We burn it to make room.

Here, the Cossacks ride. Their cloaks are heavy and their hats thick. They shave their heads so that only a single cord of herring hair remains. It is a very romantic image. Every home has a painting of Cossacks in the grass. They are heroes; we are in love with them. In the bedrooms of Ukrainian children, we tell tales of their bravery and their freedomthirst and their wide pants. In the bedrooms of Jewish children, they tell tales of their pillaging and their bloodthirst and their curved sabres. In the bedrooms of Bolshevik children, they don't talk about them at all. (For further information, Google: Decossackization.) The Cossacks ride in circles, and history is a taxi on loop. Sooner or later, you'll be guilty, too.

The grass here connects us to Crimea, the place that wasn't ours, and then was, and now no one knows. The dead poets have asked to be buried here, on a mound overlooking the Dnipro. We try to oblige.

A MILK CHURN

Put your milk inside. Put your *samizdat* inside. Bury it in the forest and hope for growth. A way of saying hello to those who come after. Notice how each one from the collective farm is numbered. Be careful: the stork is counting.

SALAMANDER

It may be a lizard, or it may be a fish. It is prehistoric. Frozen in the banks of a river. When its ancient body is uncovered in the riverbank, men rush to smash the ice. They extract it and toss it down their desperate, wolfish throats before anyone can stop them. Another writer who won the Nobel Prize has told the story, how men devour this prehistoric meat *with relish*. The river runs through Russia. Kolyma, to be exact, not far from the gulag.

COKE

It is coal, burning. It is the black earth, scorching. It is fuel. It has nothing to do with bottled corn syrup.

Our plant in Avdiyivka is the largest on the continent. It is the heart of Donbass. There is a flame at the core of the factory that must never be extinguished because it costs millions to restart that fire. Since the fighting began, this plant has been shelled 165 times. We mark them on the calendar, fold the corners to remind ourselves. The basement is a bomb shelter left over from another war. That's where the secretary's desk is now.

Sergei comes to work and is killed instantly. His father is employed here, too. He says his son liked to write poetry. It's true: you can read his poems in the newspaper. Sergei carries a notebook in his bag every day. When the shell hits, his poetry burns. They say the flame was rainbow.

A HOUSE

An imaginary thing you cannot go back to. See also "The Village (Fugue)."

RED RUE

It is worn at weddings. Suggests virginity. Its flavor is bitter. Suggests regret. To begin a sing-along for all ages, say its name, *chervona ruta*. Its name is a popular folk song about searching for the flower.

The song was written by a young medical student named Volodymyr. He is part-doctor, part-poet. His songs are secretly poems. He writes so well about our earthly things that even the Soviet radio stations can't refuse him. The radio DJs play him in Tallinn. In Vladivostok. Our language is heard across the republics. The part-doctor, part-poet is our hero; we are in love with him. Volodymyr is 30 that spring they find him hanging from a tree in the forest. The authorities rule it suicide. Of course they do.

Did I mention that you'll never find one? The flower, it's a myth. It only comes in yellow.

WHEAT

It is the golden bar at the bottom of our flag. It lines every road and window. It comes up to our bellies. As the sixth largest producer, we are world famous for it.

We have so much, but once we were starving. Starving. In 1932 the Soviets take all of it, store it in silos, guard the doors with guns, clatter their bills at boys who try to sneak some. The soldiers take it to meet state quotas, while the villagers are starving. It is five years in prison for stealing a handful. We make pancakes out of leaves, bury potato peels and hope for growth. We ground bones into flour. We take to eating cats and dogs. We take to eating bugs and flowers. If you are small enough, you take to the trees.

It seems we are always being chased into trees.

AN ALTERNATIVE STORK

In 1986, after the reactor blows up, a local child draws a picture of the bird walking through a field. Below the field is a caption: *No one told the stork.* This confuses me, because I thought it knew everything.

But another writer has already written about this. She won the Nobel Prize. I am repeating her. I am repeating myself.

A RED BEET

Blood is too easy, but what else is there to say? When we drink grandmother's *borshch,* our body temperature spikes like a dagger. It is a hot flash, though we are only children. Add an extra spoon of *smetana* cream and a sprig of dill. If that doesn't work, run to the bathroom to cool off. Fan yourself with newsprint. Splash tap water. When we spit into the sink, we will think it is our gums bleeding. Earth's most precious thing comes from inside.

SWING STATE

This one is red, communist red, the color of tomato paste and new cars. South Dakota has been easily carried by the Republicans in every election since 2000, when the color scheme of conservative "red" states and liberal "blue" states was cemented in our national consciousness. Thirteen years later, my mother, two sisters, and I are in South Dakota drinking red wine at an Italian restaurant named for a painter.

Botticelli's Ristorante is fancy by South Dakota standards ($16 linguine). Botticelli's is where we celebrate birthdays and bring out-of-town guests and where, tonight, the women of my family are having one last meal before parting ways for the school year. It is the summer of 2013, and soon I will fly to Ukraine to teach at a university in one of the country's western oblasts.

We are drinking wine in a red state, in our usual spot, but tonight there are bodyguards at the door of our small restaurant. Nearby, there is a long table of men wearing Polo shirts, and Speaker of the House John Boehner is sitting at its head. He alternates between Seafood Capellini fork twirls and smoke breaks. Every fifteen minutes John Boehner slips past our four-top and out to the dumpster alley with one of his hulking guards. Clams, Chianti, Lucky Strike. I am in awe of his tan. This man is aggressively tan. His skin, the color of afternoon tee times, his eyes, a blue I only know from cruise ship commercials.

On the sixth or seventh brush by our table, John Boehner stops and turns on unsteady feet toward my mother, the matriarch. *I just can't help but say what a fine group of ladies you have here.* He stretches out a hand to shake, his breath boozy, but we, too, have been sharing a bottle of red and are giddy at the sight of celebrity in South Dakota. There have never been guards at the door of our small restaurant before. He looks longest at my youngest sister (19 years old), the one with blue eyes to rival his own. John Boehner is drunk in a red state and very good at feigning interest: *So, what do all you lovely ladies do?* My sisters politely mention their colleges, and he seems to approve. When I tell him I'm moving to Ukraine in a few days, his cheeks drop, as if just remembering that back home in Ohio, the stove was left on.

John Boehner is caught off-guard, but he barely misses a beat. *Their president's a thug,* he says, matter-of-factly. I bristle at the word. Did he just say that? It is a loaded word and a loaded thing to say—as in, John Boehner must be loaded. I gawk at his tan, his skin the color of bronze money.

I know, I say quickly, because I don't want this man I don't know to think I don't know something.

Putin's a thug, too, he continues. *All those guys are.*

I know, I say again, though I'm not sure I do.

John Boehner glances past me, toward the *Birth of Venus* or the gondola scene or whatever is painted on the wall. His cruise-ship eyes glint with some faraway concern. Glassware pings in the background. *I'm sorry to say we've really let our in-*

terests go in the region, he mumbles, brushing against our table on his way back to the alley.

Seven months later there is the revolution, the sniper fire, the hundred dead. Yanukovych absconds and Putin sends his little green men to annex Crimea. The revolutionary chaos serves as perfect pretext for an illegal invasion. American politicians condemn Putin's land-grab, and the Kremlin responds to sanctions with sanctions of its own. Speaker of the House John Boehner is barred from entering the Russian Federation. *Proud to be included on a list of those willing to stand up to Putin's aggression,* he tweets, while John McCain jokes about not being able to summer in Siberia, so disappointed.

From my bedroom in Ukraine, I scroll John Boehner's Twitter account and remember the restaurant. I hear him again, *Putin's aggression* tucked as neatly as a shirt collar over that other uglier word. Underneath, it shrieks like a mean sunburn. John Boehner is lost at sea in a red state, he has forgotten about the stove, he looks straight through me toward the Venus on the wall. Botticelli's painted woman has legs the color of uncooked noodles and she is standing crescent-shaped on top of a scallop shell. But experts say that her posture is anatomically impossible. She could never stand like that in real life, they say. Up there, tottering on the lip of a seashell, she is impossible.

+++

After the revolution and the war, I moved to Ohio. This was like coming home, though it didn't quite feel that way. In 1988, three years before the fall of the USSR, I was born in an Ohio hospital, just 40 minutes up the road from where John Boehner and his 11 siblings grew up. I was only there for a year before my parents got divorced and my mother took me to South Dakota, the land of ponderosa pines and chokecherries.

After Ukraine, I moved back to Ohio to attend graduate school. I had lived through a revolution and a war, and I could now say, with academic smugness, that yes, Vladimir Putin is a thug. The evidence was everywhere.

I woke up one Ohio morning to the news that a prominent member of the Russian political opposition, Boris Nemtsov, had been assassinated in the night. Nemtsov had a long history of activism: protesting the use of nuclear power after Chernobyl, the war in Chechnya, and now the Russian invasion of Ukraine. But tonight—this night—he was not protesting, just strolling arm-in-arm with his Ukrainian girlfriend across Moscow's most picturesque bridge. (Is a bridge also a battlefield?) The couple was strolling in the heart of the city, shadowed by the state's red towers, when—six shots, four hits, one to the heart. A drive-by and a standard-issue Makarov pistol. Killer unknown.

When the bullet struck Nemtsov's heart, you could practically throw a stone at the Kremlin, which is like keeping your friends close and your enemies closer. When the bullet struck, most of the closed circuit cameras in the area were shut down for maintenance. Only one grainy piece of footage has been released, and at the very moment of impact, a city snowplow drives in front of the lens. There is a black market for dead dissenters.

The murder happened two days before a planned protest against the Russian war in Ukraine was to be held; Nemtsov was one of its organizers. He now lays buried in the dirt at Troyekurovskoye Cemetery, not far from Russian journalist Anna Politkovskaya. Indeed, the evidence is everywhere, I think. It is the rot they walk on.

In Ohio I also started watching the American television show *House of Cards*, about a pair of married politicians, Claire and Francis Underwood, and their ability to manipulate everyone and everything around them. Played by Robin Wright and Kevin Spacey, the Underwoods hold a simple ethic: power above all. The couple's political gains are predicated upon a dizzying arrangement of lies, bribes, and threats, and though it may be tempting to read the series as a grand analogy for the Bushes, the Clintons, or the Trumps, Francis and Claire seem rather to spotlight the most vile qualities our imaginations can conjure up for each of those powerful pairs. (These days, I am disturbed, too, at just how good Kevin Spacey was at channeling a predatory character.) Without spoiling the plot, it should surprise no one that their rule requires and justifies violence. There is much blood on the Underwoods' hands. It is a House of Rot.

By Season 3, the rotten core of the Underwood administration feels so certain to me that I am startled by the introduction of Viktor Petrov, the President of Russia and a barely veiled Vladimir Putin character. Like Putin, the fictional Petrov served abroad as a KGB agent prior to becoming president, and his rule is a brutal reflection of it. The episode "Chapter 29" has guest appearances by Nadya Tolokonnikova and Maria Alyokhina, the real-life women of Pussy Riot. Their presence acts as a sort of shorthand, reminding viewers of real-life human rights abuses in Putin's Russia.

Played by Lars Mikkelson, Viktor Petrov is perfectly gross. He is gross enough to plant an unwanted kiss on Claire Underwood's mouth in front of her husband and a room full of dignitaries during a state dinner. It is sexual assault and a political power play rolled into one. Petrov's transgression feels so vile and Claire's response so in line with what our culture demands of victims: quiet, even-tempered reproach, not a shard of self-pity, all while wearing a very flattering dress. Hers is, of course, an impossible position. In that moment, I find myself sympathizing wholly and completely with the Underwoods. In that moment, I love Claire.

Toward the end of the episode, Francis and Claire are chatting before bed and she airs her concerns about an alliance with President Petrov. Francis is frustrated at the prospect of his policy plans falling through and moves to exit the darkened bedroom. But before Francis can close the doors behind him, Claire gets the final word on Petrov.

Francis, he's a thug, she says. *Smart, but he's still a thug. Don't cower to him.* In that moment, I love Claire and do not remember the rot at all.

+++

What we need to do is understand Vladimir Putin
for what he is: a murderer and a thug.
—US Senator John McCain, CNN, February 2017

I think Vladimir Putin is a thug, a dictator, an autocratic
ruler who has his opposition killed in the streets of
Russia. He has dismembered his neighbor.
—US Senator Lindsey Graham, to reporters, September 2016

Vladimir Putin is an authoritarian thug who is accountable
to no one . . . I don't think what Vladimir Putin exhibits
is leadership. I think what he exhibits is thuggery.
—US Senator Marco Rubio, *The Guardian,* September 2016

Russia is a global menace led by a devious thug.
—Brendan Buck, Spokesperson for US House Speaker
Paul Ryan, *The Guardian,* July 2016

Putin's a former KGB agent. He's a thug. He was not elected
in a way that most people would consider a credible election
. . . I do think America is exceptional, America is different.

—US Senate Majority Leader Mitch McConnell, CNN, February 2017

I think Putin is a KGB thug.

—US Senator Ted Cruz, MSNBC, January 2017

Putin, I think, is a thug.

—Ohio Governor John Kasich, CNN, August 2016

+++

It is early October in Ohio, the only season when the sky
here looks like an ocean, endless, drowning blue. Most other
months, it is cloudy.

What do you want to do for your birthday? my new boyfriend asks. His name is Christopher and he is like that: the
kind of man who will carry a child across a river. The kind of
man who instinctively knows when there's a child who needs
carrying. He is from Ohio and very patient when I complain
about how much I hate the weather here.

I have not thought much about my birthday this year, except for the fact that it is also a death day. On October 7, 2006,
Russian journalist Anna Politkovskaya returned to her Moscow
apartment building after grocery shopping. She stepped into
the elevator, and behind her a man dressed in black. (Is an elevator also a war?) Four shots, one to the head, and a standard-
issue Makarov pistol. The assassin left her crumpled on the
ground like a pile of dead, wet leaves, a heap of rotten leaves.

Anna was a critic of the Kremlin's war in Chechnya. It is an old story. (In fact, Boris Nemtsov attended Anna's funeral, accompanying her body toward its final dirt at Troyekurovskoye, not knowing—though, perhaps, also knowing—that soon it would be his dirt as well.) This year, October 7, 2016, is the tenth anniversary of her murder.

I have not thought about my birthday, but I have been thinking a lot about Anna. I have been reading her books and articles about the Russian government's violence in Chechnya, and I pretend we are having conversations, like an interview in reverse:

> What did you see in Chechnya?
> *A young woman called Sina is having a seizure.*
> What happened?
> *Mass poisonings at schools in the Shelkovsk region.*
> How is she doing?
> *Her brother unclenches her teeth with a spoon.*
> And now?
> *The girl is now bent in an impossible arch, her heels touching the back of her head.*

When I read Anna's words, I cry. I begin to think that my birthday only matters because it leaves me feeling convicted. She is a much better writer than I could ever hope to be. She is dead, and I am alive.

I want to do something for Anna, I tell Chris. *That's what I want this year.*

+++

It is early October 2016 and we cannot turn off our news feeds. The first woman and the first reality TV star are running against each other for president of the United States. It is spectacle like I have never seen. On my birthday, the *Washington Post* will release a recording of presidential candidate Donald Trump in a private conversation. *I better use some Tic Tacs just in case I start kissing her,* he says. *You know I'm automatically attracted to beautiful—I just start kissing them. It's like a magnet. Just kiss. I don't even wait. And when you're a star, they let you do it. You can do anything. Grab 'em by the pussy. You can do anything.* Surely, I think, anyone who cares about the well-being of women cannot support this man.

Earlier in the campaign, a name I recognized from the river emerged once again: Paul Manafort. Trump hired Manafort in March to manage the convention and later promoted him to campaign chairman. The man who had advised Yanukovych through years of bumbling despotism—through the betrayal at Vilnius, through the switched bullet barrels, the sniper fire, the hundred dead on Maidan—was now advising the Republican presidential nominee. When news of Manafort's vast sums of laundered Ukrainian income broke in August, Manafort officially resigned from Trump's campaign, though his resignation does little to ease my concern about his involvement in the first place. Once drawn, I cannot shake the parallel between Yanukovych and Trump.

I am disturbed, too, at the things Trump says about Vladimir Putin, which do not reflect what seems to be the official party stance on the Russian president's thuggery. Trump says that Putin is *doing a great job* and that *in terms of leadership he is getting an 'A.'* He shrugs off accusations that Putin is responsible for the murder of journalists. *Have you been able to prove that? Do you know the names of the reporters that he's killed?* He also vacillates wildly on the very state of their relationship, saying nine times publicly that he and Putin have met or spoken (that, in fact, they *got along great!*), and later denying any contact was made. *I have never met Putin . . . I don't know who Putin is.*

These facts terrify me. I feel as if I am looking backward and forward at once, as if history is on loop. I recall my students and coworkers in Ukraine, how during the winter revolution, they took their bodies to the center of the capital. They took their down feather coats and their scarves and their bodies, and this was meaningful—their bodies at the heart of the city. In response, the Ukrainian president fled in his helicopter. He ran away to Russia.

I am angry that Anna is dead, and I am angry that Trump is a candidate, and I am angry that Vladimir Putin and I share a birthday: October 7th. I ask Chris if we can protest in downtown Columbus, Ohio, on that day, if we can make some sort of small demonstration to tell people about Anna Politkovskaya because *isn't it a shame that people don't know her? Plus this is a swing state! Maybe we can reason with them . . .* It is an odd birthday request, but Chris doesn't act like it. He returns from a nearby print shop with a picket sign of Anna Politkovskaya's face and another of Putin holding a baby Trump, made in the style of a classic Soviet propaganda poster originally featuring Joseph Stalin. The flag baby Trump waves is communist red, the color of new cars, and the background is blue as a river.

+++

Trump. Hillary. Anna. A young woman. Putin. Petrov. Claire. Nadya. Maria. Anna. Putin. Trump. Hillary. Young woman. Putin. Boehner. Botticelli. Maria. Nadya. My sisters. Anna. Hillary. Claire. Petrov. Putin. Trump. Kasich. Rubio. Cruz. Putin. Petrov. My mother. Nadya. Maria. Claire. Hillary. Anna. Woman.

+++

We select the most prominent corner in town, the corner of Broad and High. Across the street we can see the Greek lime-stone columns of the Ohio Statehouse, where Governor Kasich has his office. They rise like white towers above the buses, and trash, and businesspeople of Ohio's capital city. The sun today is too high for shadows.

We hold our picket signs and pass out informational bro-chures: *Today is the 10th anniversary of Anna Politkovskaya's assassination . . . 34 journalists have been murdered since Putin was inaugurated in 2000 . . . presidential candidate Donald Trump admires Vladimir Putin's leadership . . . is this what lead-ership means to you?*

I fact-check the brochure obsessively before printing it. (Several Russian journalists have been murdered since 2016, bringing the total to 37, though that number is conservative.) I do not want a stranger to have any leverage over me because of a slippery fact. I read, and re-read, and check, and re-check; I include a long list of citations on the back page. I am ready to combat any stranger's whataboutism with plain facts. For example: According to the Committee to Protect Journalists, six American journalists were murdered during that same time frame.

On the corner of Broad and High, some people take our brochures reluctantly. Some shake their heads at us. A few stop and chat, enthused by our strange little project. Thank you for informing people, they say. He is a dangerous man, they say. But this is still months before the question of Trump's Russia "collusion" will dominate the front page, so most people just ignore us. It is a Friday, after all, and it is beautiful and who can be bothered with dead Russians on such a beautiful Friday afternoon?

I do feel a little foolish there on the corner, but truly, the weather could not be better. It is warm, more like August than October. The sky is some foreign shade of blue, the sort of Crimean blue that makes you gasp when you see it up close. Perhaps the sky looks this way because a frame of leaves serves as its contrast: burning orange and red. We are lucky today, I think. It is a good birthday.

You guys are retarded. A man in a pinstripe suit approaches us. He is yelling.

You are such retards! Really, such retards. I look around the sidewalk. Who is he talking to? The man points his phone at our corner.

You Americans are so brainwashed, he continues. *It is absolutely unbelievable.* And I cannot believe this grown man. I swing my head around to the politicians and corporate types taking lunch. Do they hear pinstripe's shouting, too? Perhaps I am imagining this interaction, like I imagine the young woman with a spoon in her mouth. *Honestly, the brainwashing here is unbelievable! You guys are completely retarded.* He is standing beside a woman in a business skirt and jacket. They are smiling and laughing, as if the solemn portrait of the late Anna Politkovskaya on a picket sign is a joke. Perhaps they are amused by the word he keeps repeating. It takes a long moment before I realize: they both have Russian accents.

I would appreciate if you didn't use that word, Chris says, calm as ever. I am too stunned to speak.

Okay, okay, but you guys are still retards, the man says. He and the woman huddle close. They switch to Russian and snicker as they walk away, slipping into the midday crowd of Americans.

I am shaking. The word burns. I expected to meet an angry Trump supporter or two. I expected to explain that six American journalists have been killed, that these are Trump's direct quotes from interviews. But here, in *the heart of it all!,* I did not expect to meet an angry Putin supporter. Chris tells me not to worry about the Russian couple, and I try not to, though by now I imagine our photo splayed all over VKontakte, Russian Facebook, with some cruel caption. Stupid Americans.

It is lunchtime in the center of this great swing state, and there are still brochures to disseminate, discomforts to inflict or bear. Some passersby take our brochure reluctantly, some shake their heads, some stop and chat, enthused by our strange little project. After maybe 45 minutes, the Russian couple walks back by our spot on the sidewalk. They say goodbye to each other, and the man crosses the street, still clearly amused by us. The woman lingers on our corner for a moment. I wonder if maybe she wants to talk.

Hi, my name is Sonya, I hold out my hand. She is suspicious, but takes it. *Can you tell us what is upsetting you?* I ask.

You just don't understand how brainwashed you are, she says. Her voice is shivering, like a leaf. *This—these 34 journalists, this Politkovskaya—this has nothing to do with Putin. Why are you standing here?*

Have you read Anna's books? I ask.

No, she says.

They are good . . . But they are scary. I'm scared that one of our presidential candidates admires a man who has created such a hostile environment in Russia . . . I don't want that to happen here.

The woman glances up at Anna. Her eyes are shining, like maybe she will cry. *But don't you know? This is the least free country I have ever been in,* she says.

I pause for a moment and wonder who she is and why she is here. *I know we have a lot of problems,* I say, *but at least we are able to stand on this corner for a few hours before getting hauled away.* I gesture up at the Statehouse building, the way my friends in Belarus used to point to the ceiling whenever they talked about the dictator. *Could you do this in Moscow?* I ask.

The Russian woman ignores my question. *This is not a free country. For example, the food here is not good. It is not fresh. Back in Russia our food is really very fresh.*

There are many different kinds of food here, I say. I am calculating. Perhaps a concession will help my argument. And, I suppose, she is not completely wrong. *Yes, it's true some people don't have access to fresh food.*

She is emboldened. *Have you ever been to the bus station here?* She nods toward the Greyhound hub a few blocks away. *It is really unbelievable how poor people are. It is so dirty.* I stare at the Russian woman's face. She is beautiful, with slender features, and sleek hair, and wide, blue eyes. Her pencil skirt slinks around her long figure. Her cheeks are rouged. She is curved as a Gothic ivory and graceful in high heels. This is something I secretly envy about Eastern European women. They have trained themselves to make stilettos seem like a natural state. Like we were born to stand this way, relaxed on twin daggers. The Russian woman looks down at me.

I have been to the bus station, I tell her. *But I'm not sure how that's relevant.*

Well, she goes on, *I have been all over the world, and this is definitely the least free country.*

We stand on the corner of Broad and High, me and this aggressively beautiful Russian woman. I feel like a child there in my American jeans and sandals. She soars above in those elegant shoes, somehow both at ease and unfamiliar, as if a soft wind has only just now delivered her to this strange land. We stare into each other's eyes. Maybe, if we stare long enough, we can understand the Cold War. Maybe our worldviews will collude and catch fire and melt together. I am shaking, and I think she is, too. We are tottering. Her blue eyes fill with water, and so do mine. We are lost at sea, sailing in mad circles, groping for the next word of attack. There is a sound of seagulls, or city pigeons. The sidewalk is capsized. I worry we will both drown.

We look nothing alike, me and the Russian woman, but for one quick moment, it is like peering into uncanny glass. I see myself, though I know this is impossible.

+++

That same weekend, after the release of the *Access Hollywood* tape featuring presidential candidate Donald Trump, I stay in bed and read about the women who have accused him of sexual assault.

Natasha Stoynoff says Trump pushed her up against a wall and shoved his tongue down her throat. Kristin Anderson says Trump reached up her skirt and touched her. Rachel Crooks says Trump introduced himself and then kissed her on the lips outside an elevator. Jessica Leeds says Trump groped her on an airplane. Summer Zervos says Trump kissed her on the lips twice when they met to discuss her employment options. Ninni Laaksonen says Trump touched her backside before a Miss Universe appearance. Jill Harth says Trump forced her into a bedroom where he groped and kissed her. Temple Taggart says Trump kissed her on the lips when they first met. Mindy McGillivray says Trump grabbed her backside at Mar-a-Lago. Cassandra Searles says Trump grabbed her backside as well. Karena Virginia says Trump touched her breast. Jessica Drake says Trump kissed her without permission. Cathy Heller says Trump grabbed her and kissed her in front of her family.

I think about these women often. I did not learn the Russian woman's name from that cloudless Friday, but I think about her, too. Does she consider me? My jeans, and my picket signs, and my green convictions? How wrong, how right we both were?

+++

A month after Vladimir Putin's 64th birthday, Ohio went red and Donald Trump won the election. We elected our very own television president.

Chris and I attended an election night party at a friend's apartment in Columbus. Halfway through the night, two friends showed up very drunk, and it occurred to me that perhaps they knew something I didn't. As the results crept into the room, we decided to leave for home. *It was like the Titanic in there*, Chris said. *Like a party turned into a sinking ship.*

I remember standing in the alley behind my house that night. It was dark. I didn't feel like passing through the gate into my backyard, or moving out onto the well-lit street. I stood in the drowning gloom of the alley. I just stood there, in between.

+++

Sometime after the inauguration, I attended a reading given by Yale historian and Eastern European specialist Timothy Snyder. During the Q&A session, I asked if he thinks it's a good idea for Americans to call Putin a "thug" with such ease and regularity: *The term kind of flatters us, doesn't it?* Snyder said. *Vladimir Putin is the leader of a modern, functioning authoritarian regime with broad popular support from his countrymen.*

I asked Russian-American journalist Masha Gessen a similar question at a book signing a few months later: *Well,* she laughed. *Considering I pretty much coined this usage of it while on tour with that book*—she pointed to a copy of her other book, the one with Putin's face on it—*I guess I can't complain too much.*

I met Pussy Riot member Maria Alyokhina in real life and brought it up again, this question that's become my obsession, this word I haven't been able to shake since the Italian restaurant over five years ago: *What do you mean "thug"?* she replied.

Like gangster, mafia man, I said.

Well, he is a mafia man. It is a mafia state.

So you think the term is accurate? I looked into the blue eyes of this woman who spent two years in a Russian prison colony. Two years in a cold cell, its wall cracks stuffed with chewed bread and sanitary napkins. The balls of dough and cheap pads were for insulation, left behind by another woman. Maria lived in a cold cell, thousands of kilometers from her young son, and was subjected to regular "gynecological searches."

Yes, she said. *It is accurate.*

At one lecture, NPR foreign correspondent Anne Garrels answered my question without my prompting it: *The thing is, Vladimir Putin is a thug.* She paused for a fugitive moment and gazed out at the room of American academics. *But he's their thug.*

The etymology of the word has been traced to India, to the Hindi word for swindler, which in turn may have something to do with the Sanskrit verb to cover, or to conceal. British colonial accounts use the word to describe a group of Indian bandits that were said to engage in human sacrifice and highway robbery. (Predictably, these accounts offer no legitimate grievance as explanation.) In American hip-hop culture the word maintains a connotation of resilience in the face of adversity and racism. It is tough, but loveable. And when some Americans use it—often to complain about protestors or rioters—it serves, arguably, as a stand-in for the N-word.

Like all words, this one is in perpetual motion, moving through continents and meanings. I try to pin it down, but it flits across the water. At times it motors, and at times it floats. It rocks back and forth, shrinking from view and ballooning again. I hear it in John Boehner's mouth. In Claire Underwood's. In Anne Garrels's. Some days I think yes, it is right, this is the one, and other days it eludes certainty. I blink. The word is a cover, a way to conceal, a distraction. A shirt collar tucked neatly. I blink again. The winds change, and it is gone.

+++

Chris and I recently moved to a blue state. We did not move to a blue state on purpose but it was, we thought, a not entirely unpleasant consequence of having to relocate for a new job. We live by the ocean now and like to watch boats scudding through the canal on sunny afternoons. There is same-day fish for sale everywhere. We are eating oysters raw. It is nice here, though I won't be surprised if someday we move back to Ohio. Or even back to my home state, South Dakota, its ponderosa pines and chokecherries.

Anna Politkovskaya has been dead 12 years now, and sometimes our conversations turn to the Russian couple, the weather that day.

You were so upset, Chris reminds me.

I was so confused, I say, which means I couldn't tell where the Russian woman ended, or where I began.

When we packed boxes to leave Ohio, I found the picket signs from our little protest still in the basement, pinched beneath some old rugs and a broken Swiffer. I didn't have the heart to throw the signs in the dumpster. Instead, I stuck the late Anna Politkovskaya's face in the yard, on the side you can see from one of Columbus's busiest streets. My old roommate called a few weeks after we left and said a man had come to the door of the house, spitting mad. The man wanted to know who put the sign there. He was furious, my roommate reported, and he had an accent. I feel guilty for putting my roommate in that situation. Who am I to wave such a picket sign anyway? Since Trump was inaugurated, five American journalists have been murdered, nearly doubling the national total. A newsroom has always been a frontline.

Which reminds me: I read recently that Rachel Crooks, one of the women who accused Donald Trump of sexual assault, won a Democratic primary for the Ohio State Legislature. She decided to enter politics after the man who forcibly kissed her outside an elevator was elected President of the United States. Yes, sometimes an elevator is a war.

But that is happening in Ohio, and we are in a blue state now. Our new blue state home is also home to my Ukrainian godmother. A few days before my birthday, she and I go for a walk around a nearby lake. My godmother is a painter and art historian, and we talk about the *Birth of Venus.*

Contrapasso? I say. *Is that the word for her posture?*

Contrapposto, she corrects me. *It's a classical pose. One leg engaged, the other free.* My godmother pauses for a moment, slows her walk. The lake purls beside us. It is not blue at all. It is black and sunless. *I haven't thought about that painting in years.*

Contrapposto means that Venus is curved, like a clump of linguini stuck to the sink. Her right leg is bent and relaxed.

Her left leg is at work, supporting the weight of her body. It is a stance of productive tension. She is at rest and in motion, both at once. And her particular version of the posture is extreme, her neck too long, experts say, its existence unlikely. This unfeasible woman, half-at ease, half-surging.

The Italian word *contrapposto* is derived from the Latin *contrapositum*, which means antithesis. It is related to another word, a verb, *contrapono*. To set against. To pit against. To oppose. Botticelli's painted lady holds an impossible position. She is at war with herself.

And she is stuck there, warring on the wall of the Uffizi Gallery, caged in a gilded frame. When Venus gets tired, she can't shift legs. She can't seesaw, like the rest of us. The rest of us, arranged neatly on the sidewalks of the world; decorating the back rooms of restaurants; groping about the alleys. The rest of us are scoping street corners like a thousand tiny battlefields. We search for another face to stare down, a small cement valley in between. It is our own reflection caught in a pane of glass. Uncanny, we think, before swaying to check if it moves.

THE VILLAGE (REPRISE)

When we return, it's a Sunday.

I am with Chris and two American friends, the summer of 2017. I set an alarm to wake everyone up because we are hungover. We had spent the night before at a dance party in Lviv, an open-air disco under the stars. The DJ party was held in the Park of Culture and Recreation, *Park Kultury,* a place established by the Soviets and which once hosted magnificent agricultural exhibits: the latest milk processors, the best methods for tilling, rows of polished tractors. Not far from where the tractors used to gather, we danced to a mixture of funk and electronica, most of it in English. We drank Aperol Spritz near the fire pit. We shared a charcuterie under string lights. Every detail seemed curated for Instagram. And though the event was outside, its organizers ensured electrical outlets, for guests to charge their devices, would be available.

We stayed late. Two young women from Crimea told us they couldn't go home. They looked like twins, these two Crimean women each wearing two braids. The dance floor was made of packed sand, and it was difficult to hear them over the music. But I think that's what they said—that they couldn't go home. Or, they didn't want to.

There used to be twin statues here in the park, near where we were dancing and nibbling smoked meats. Stalin and Lenin. They faced each other. But those were torn down years ago. I ordered another Spritz.

When we paid admission to the outdoor club, a man snapped a wristband on my arm. It was white and black and said, IN FUTURE WE TRUST, just like that, in block English letters. On the morning we are supposed to go to the village, I wake with dents in my skin from the plastic band. I consider cutting it off, but I like how the words look there on my arm. I am too woozy to think very hard about why this might be, beyond the fact that I am a glutton for metaphor. A lush, you could say.

I am with Chris and two American friends and our middle-aged driver, Bohdan. Our ship is Bohdan's Mercedes van, which he uses to drive heritage tourists like myself from Lviv to their ancestral Ukrainian villages. And he is well practiced in this, I can tell, because he steers marvelously around the country's tire-collapsing potholes. As we drive, I promise myself I will never write about the country's tire-collapsing potholes. I will never be responsible for recording that cliché. But now I am far away, and I can't ignore our flitting back and forth. We head north to the village, meandering all the way, and I think of a line by Ilya Kaminsky that I found once in a bookstore: *We lived north of the future.* Bohdan drives northward, expertly missing all the worst potholes.

Somewhere in the middle of our trip, near the meeting corner of three oblasts, Bohdan puts a CD into the car stereo. The sound is spilling over with keyboards and synthesizers, and it is catchy. It feels like the long-ago 1980s, but also like an indie band I heard on Pitchfork recently. *This is me,* Bohdan says. *I am the drummer.* He speaks to me in Ukrainian, though the song's lyrics are Russian.

What was your band name? I ask.

The Seasons, he says.

Wow, the recording is really professional, Chris says to me.

Were you famous? I ask Bohdan.

Yes, we were pretty famous. But that was long ago.

We ooo and ahh over Bohdan, our famous drummer-driver. He is very good at navigating the country's tire-collapsing potholes and he is very good, it seems, at keeping a beat. We love the music. We love the field of poppies facing us out the eastside van window. We love our Soviet rockstar. Chris is also a musician, and so I translate his eager questions for Bohdan.

Do you still play drums? I ask.

No, Bohdan says. *Now I have three vans and three children.*

The day is bright and balmy. We stop the van near one of the poppy fields for a photo session (*a fotosessiya,* we joke). We have another *fotosessiya* in front of the village welcome sign. Another in front of a loose horse. In one small town, our van is stopped by a glut of people processing slowly down the main road. We gawk at their medieval-looking pants. My American friend holds her cellphone to the windshield and snaps a series of pictures. Bohdan looks at her. *You might not want to do that,* he says. *It's a funeral.*

Even if my eyes were closed, I would know the village by how the road feels under our vehicle. This one is not potholed, but cobblestoned. The stones jut at weird angles, and flitting back and forth won't do much good. To get to the village you have to creep. Creep like bad news into a room, or like snakes.

We pull up to Marina's house, the trees in front slumped under fruit. Her nephew Yarosh greets us at the gate and ushers us into the living room. Though I told him we would be bringing food and not to prepare anything, Yarosh ignored my request. Inside, a fine Ukrainian table has been laid: fresh cut tomatoes, cucumbers, radish, sliced bread, jugs of *uzvar*, two kinds of *kolbasa* sausage, Yarosh's own *samohon* moonshine, shot glasses, a tablecloth of roses, individually wrapped ice cream bars, and last year's pig in lard. The walls of Marina's house are rainbow, jewel-tones, embroidery, an intricate textile on the couch. St. Volodymyr shines golden in the corner. I am giddy to find the house just as I remembered. *Do you think Marina would sell me that?* my American friend points to a neon cross-stich on the wall. *Shh,* I say. Everything is perfect as it is.

But where's Marina? I ask Yarosh.

She's sleeping, he says. *In the bedroom.*

Can I see her?

We can see her later, he tells me.

Please?

Fine, ok.

It is gloomy in the room where she sleeps, and I can barely spot Marina's four-and-a-half-foot frame, skeletal under a heap of rugs and blankets. It is June, and she looks freezing. *Marina, we have company,* Yarosh nudges her. Her eyes crack like clay. She has just woken from an ancient dream. Marina searches my face, groping for its meaning. I explain who I am to her, how this is my fourth visit to her beautiful home and how I was here last time three years ago, how Nina her cousin is my beloved late Busia, and how the whole American family sends their regards. She smiles. My explanation grows thin and specious the longer it hangs there. I notice a smell of bad eggs. *It's good to see you,* I say. Marina does not recognize me, but has, rather, the studious look of someone wanting to recognize.

We partake of the table all afternoon. In fine Ukrainian table fashion, Yarosh leads us in a series of toasts—to our meeting!—between bites of food. The moonshine is clean and strong, like swallowing glass. After the first shot, Chris gasps a little, *That must be 180 proof.* He barely has time to catch his breath before

I am translating Yarosh's next toast—between the first and second a bullet should not pass!—and we send it splashing down our throats. Bud'mo!! Last year's pig is rich and fatty. I gum a slice of sausage. It would be nice to chase the shine, but my father has warned me about the prune juice.

> *That fresh-squeezed prune juice'll give you the* **runs,** he said, recalling a visit he made to the village in the '90s. *And there's no toilet,* he continued, *you have to use the field.* Busia was with him on that trip, her first and only trip back to Ukraine.

They are pouring another shot—to family!—and I am instantly swimmy.

> Busia said when they returned she didn't recognize the place. *There used to be hills and forest and big river, Ikva.*

Hiccup. Bud'mo! I ball a piece of bread and suck the moisture out. It is a relief to taste.

> Busia said now everything is small, and flat, and the forest stripped bare. It is a different village. *Is your house still there?* I asked her.

My shotglass is full again. One of the Americans rubs her hands together in anticipation. *Yarosh, I'm sorry,* I say, *but I have to slow down,* and I think my boyfriend is waving in agreement. *Po p'yatdesyat,* Yarosh begs, just another 50 milliliters, one more shot. He holds his pointer finger in a hook shape, bent like a hangman's gallows, and wags it at us. Ukrainian hospitality is gluttonous.

> *No,* Busia laughed, as if the answer were obvious and I a fool for asking, *our houses are all gone. Nema, vse.*

We tip our crystal bottoms up—to country!—and this time I douse the vodka burn in cut tomatoes. The Americans have their cameras out. *This backdrop is so good,* one says to the other. Bud'mo.

After how many shots—to women, to love, to the dead—I cannot say, we decide it is time for fresh air. Bohdan, who wisely declined all of the booze, agrees a walk would be a good idea. Marina follows us out of the house, too. She does not seem to want to join our impromptu tour, but moves instead like someone lost. She wanders about the yard, as we stroll the village.

Yarosh takes us to see this year's pig in the stable behind his house. The pig is a mad, honking creature and it charges us. When Yarosh tries to corral it back into the pen with a stick, this year's pig knocks him over. I have a looming sense that maybe we are a little too drunk. I am embarrassed on Yarosh's behalf, but he laughs it off. We stop next by the village cemetery to admire its eggshell-blue headstones and neon fabric flowers. Here, Bohdan and Yarosh have a serious conversation about the war.

Have you lost anyone yet? Bohdan says, meaning the collective *you.* We are stopped in front of a Soviet-era memorial to the victims of World War II.

No, Yarosh says. *Thanks be to God. The next village, yes, but here not. Thanks be to God.* We all nod solemnly.

Yarosh walks us back by Marina's house. I admire the lush potato field beside it. *Who planted all these?* I ask. Yarosh answers, *I did, of course . . . But they are not so great this year. We have big problem with Koloradi.* We get closer, and I see the potato rows are creeping. The leaves are shuddering under a small army of orange-and-black-striped bugs. I watch one beetle eat the scorched leaf beneath itself. It is nibbling away at the very thing holding it up.

Why Koloradi? Are they from Colorado? I ask.

I guess so, Yarosh says.

Or from Russia, Bohdan jokes. He is referring to the Russian-backed separatists in Eastern Ukraine, some of whom don the orange-and-black-striped ribbon of St. George. The ribbon is an old Russian Imperial military symbol that has been revived in the new war. It has become a shorthand for the occupation itself, and *Koloradi* a derogatory term for pro-Russian militants. During the Cold War, the communist states of Europe declared the Colorado beetle a grand CIA plot. They said the US government would infest a field overnight, dropping the bug from an airplane. Authorities enlisted children to help pick the beetles off, one by one. *You know,* I say to nobody in particular, *my home state in America is very close to Colorado.* Yarosh and Marina have never been to America. They have never been to Lviv.

Yarosh walks us past the potatoes, past the bugs, and back into someone else's field, about 300 yards from the road. *This is where your grandmother's house used to be.* I stand in the middle of a green lot, face bare to the sun, elbows exposed, the disco wristband reflecting a sharp glare. IN FUTURE WE TRUST. I am standing there in a pair of black, orthopedic Reebok shoes that I took from Busia's house after she died. We had the same size feet, and I am a lush. I think about Busia's jars of soil hidden in the closet and the soil under my sneakers now. I am standing in the middle of someone else's field. This plot of land was probably seized by the authorities and designated for a collective farm after we left. I am standing barefaced in someone else's field, next to an imaginary house. There is nothing here now but dirt or sky. There is nothing here but me.

I want to stand in the field all afternoon, a woman caught in a painting. Here, I am a symbol. I relish the metaphor I am, standing where the house used to be. The house is gone and Busia is gone, but I am here in her soil-black shoes. I am mushrooming up from the dirt like a *sonyashnyk*, a sunflower face. I am a reflection, casting backward and forward and back again. I can't say where Busia ends, or I begin.

Back in the living room, we sit down for round two of our fine Ukrainian table, but I can see Marina is displeased. The mood in the house has shifted, as if some disturbed current invaded the space in our absence. Marina's eyes get very wide. *Who are you? I don't know who you are,* she says to me when I try again to explain. *I don't know you.* Yarosh tries to explain as well—about Busia, about the family in America, about how this is my fourth visit to her beautiful home—but these references to the past do not cue anything inside her. Marina is more frustrated the longer she puzzles over my strange face. *I live alone,* she says. *No one lives here but me.* Her eyeballs are huge, like they could swallow her head, magnified by thick spectacles. I am also wearing glasses. We share bad eyes. *Did you just come here to laugh at me?* she asks. I am hurt by her words and glad that Chris and the Americans don't understand them. *I don't know who you are, but you need to leave.* Marina coughs at me like a scrap caught in her throat, an unpleasant bit of bone she just wants to swallow already, just swallow and be done with already. *I live alone.*

Chris cannot translate her words, but he senses something is wrong. He gestures to our American friends and they all stumble away from the house in an attempt to restore peace. I tell Marina that I'm so sorry for upsetting her and then back away slowly myself. Yarosh explains that Marina is elderly and senile and probably has dementia and that we shouldn't take it personally and that sometimes she gets confused and agitated and it's no big deal, really. I understand what Yarosh is saying, but it doesn't change how I feel. His explanation does about as much good for me as my explanation did for Marina. Busia's village has suddenly gone dim. They do not want me here. They do not need me. I am a crest of fat, guilty tears.

I tell Yarosh that we should get going, though he won't stand for it. He insists we let Marina sleep and continue our reunion down the road at his house. He brings the *samohon* to smooth things over, but all I want is to cry and throw up. Glass sloshes in my stomach. I translate a few more toasts for the group, but refuse to drink them, and as the others are saying their good-byes, I slide a thick stack of rainbow-stained bills under a plastic bag in the corner. Yarosh will find my guilt offering in a day or two. The money poets scowl at me, as I proceed to do what all the other family members have always done and what I have also, always, done—which is leave.

We load up our Soviet rockstar van and flit back and forth toward the future.

+++

Six months later I am just waking up in an American blue state. I put on the kettle and look outside to the gray. Behind me, there is kombucha in the fridge. Organic bread on the shelf. A locally distilled spirit on the counter. There is a record player and a bookshelf with names like Dostoevsky, Zagajewski, Heschel, Zhadan. One red book, even, with my own name on the spine. Somewhere, a can of sparkling water sits half drunk.

The teakettle begins to rattle. I prepare a cup of pour-over coffee, beans roasted not far from this very apartment. I scan the day's *New York Times* headlines with intent smugness.

IN EASTERN EUROPE, POPULISM LIVES, WIDENING A
SPLIT IN THE E.U.
JUSTICES SEEM READY TO LIMIT WHISTLE-BLOWERS
PROTECTIONS.
ODDS ARE, RUSSIA OWNS TRUMP.

The headlines make me angry, but I notice that, on certain days, it slips into a self-satisfied sort of anger. I get to be angry because I am a person *in the know*. I read about political candidates, and I sign petitions, and sometimes I even attend protests. I have grown up so much since my time in Ukraine, in Belarus. Now, I have a graduate degree. This pour-over coffee tastes delicious, I think, taking a long, satisfied sip. And I am very well informed.

After a few minutes with the headlines, I click over to my email tab. A message in bold: **відповідь на заяву.** Is it . . . ?

Yes. Yes, I have been waiting for this. A message from the Ukrainian archives. I have requested documents related to my great-grandfather's arrest because I am trying to pin down the timeline. I cannot believe the archivist responded so quickly. With digital copies straight to my inbox! The answers right here! The screen light reflecting off my face, I begin to translate, slowly, one word at a time.

> Criminal Case № XXXXX.
> Born 1887.
> Wife.
> Children.
> Nina.
> Germany.
> Occupation.
> Village Elder.
> Wehrmacht.
> 50 Inhabitants.
> 46 Inhabitants.
> 55 Inhabitants.
> 7 Activists.
> Betrayal.
> Accomplice.
> Enemy.

Letters drop like a waterfall. I am chasing them backwards, up to their source, scrambling, clawing, gnashing of teeth, gnawing down my fingernails one at a time, tears cresting, fat, falling. A box of old toenails spills on the floor. We try not to look down there. Down the hill, down into the ravine. The room is a pit of creeping snakes. Gloating crows.

Down,
down,
down.

The words curl over me as a skull.

+++

According to the archive documents, my great-grandfather Joseph was, indeed, taken by the NKVD, the Bolsheviks, the *bad men* Busia had warned me about. He was arrested in 1944 after Soviet troops reclaimed western Ukraine, sat trial in early 1945, was found guilty and sentenced to 20 years hard labor in a Siberian gulag. In the gulag camp at Taishet (which means "cold river" in Ket, a native Siberian language), most prisoners worked building the railroad or logging trees. They cut timber for twelve hours a day and sometimes were given only horse feed to eat. "We have to squeeze everything out of a prisoner in the first three months," Alexander Solzhenitsyn recorded one gulag administrator saying. "After that, we don't need him anymore." My great-grandfather died in the summer of 1945, having barely arrived at the camp.

My mouth hangs open like an unhinged gate. Men are taken from their own yards, loaded into cattle cars. They peel their sticky limbs off one another for the 3,000-mile journey to Taishet. Workers collapse on either side of Joseph. Tell yourself it's just buckwheat. It's buckwheat. It's buckwheat.

I am horrified to have Joseph's suffering confirmed, even though I know this is precisely what I was looking for. I wanted some sign of our victimhood. Disturbing as it is, my great-grandfather's deportation fits neatly with what I expected to find.

But as I continue translating, something strange—a little hic-cup—emerges.

It is written in the archive documents that Joseph was a *starosta,* or village elder, under the administration of the German occupiers.

I pause here, unsure of what to make of this note. I grasp for the village timeline: Okay, up until 1939, the village is more or less under Polish rule. There is that one front Busia mentioned that forced her parents to evacuate for a while. That must have been around 1915. Then in 1939 the Soviets and Germans divvied up Poland between them, and the Soviets were granted control of the village. In 1941 the Germans broke the pact and invaded the village. In 1944 the Soviets drove the Germans out of the re-gion and retook the village. In 1991 the USSR fell and the village became part of independent Ukraine, making it 27 years old, which is younger than me, sitting here in my blue state apart-ment, translating archive documents.

So, Joseph was a *starosta* during the German occupation. I had heard that he was considered an honorary village mayor during the time of Polish rule, though he was not particularly loyal to the Poles, and was certainly not loyal to the Soviets who came afterward, since both groups oppressed Ukrainians. By this point, he was, essentially, a stateless man, and a stateless man is a weak man. Perhaps it was not such a stretch to coop-erate with an invading empire, to hold out hope that this one might be a little better than the last? Perhaps the Nazis wanted continuity, and he was given no choice in the matter at all.

I read on. The documents claim Joseph handed over five ri-fles and a machine gun to the Germans, and that his horse was used in a convoy sent to collect ammunition from local villag-ers. The *starosta,* I learn elsewhere, is primarily an economic role, concerned with ensuring the Germans received whatever goods they needed from the occupied territories. And, in terms of economics, what the Third Reich most desperately needed from Ukraine was *labor*. According to the trial papers, Joseph was also accused of being involved in sending away residents from the village. The villagers were shipped to Germany, where they worked as forced laborers, *ostarbeiters*, fulfilling wartime labor quotas. The records allege that he helped with three shipments of eastern workers, one shipment of 50 people, then 46 people, then 55.

Hiccup. I begin to feel queasy. How can this be, these shipments? He was forced to meet quotas. Or, perhaps he thought sending Ukrainians away from the Russian sphere was not such a bad thing after all, that there was still some hope to be had in the "progress" of European civilization. By this time the Germans had disseminated propaganda posters across Ukraine, boasting of favorable work conditions and high pay (though, such rosy pictures did not hold up upon arrival in Nazi Germany). Maybe, like the *Banderivtsi*, Joseph felt this was the best bet for eventual Ukrainian independence. Maybe he figured cooperation with the occupier would spare the lives of his wife and five children. As historian Orest Subtelny notes, during a military occupation, "from an average individual's point of view, success generally meant the preservation of one's life." And, especially in Ukraine, preservation of life was not a given. According to Timothy Snyder, "between 1933 and 1945 there was no more dangerous place in the world than Ukraine. More people were killed as a result of policy in Ukraine than anywhere else in the world . . ." Or, maybe, it was just a war and if Stanley Milgram taught us anything, it is that we are all much more deferential to authority than we think.

I am eager to give Joseph the benefit of the doubt because he is family, and what is family good for if not that? No one has ever uttered an unkind word about him.

I turn back to the computer screen and continue translating: my great-grandfather is charged with informing police about seven local communist activists. The seven activists were detained and killed by Gestapo.

There is kombucha in my fridge, and seven people were killed by Gestapo. The absurd is not just a literary device or a political tactic. It is a blue state installed on stolen lands. It is this gray morning. It is *me*.

There is no reasoning away the Gestapo, and so all I can do for a long time is weep. I cannot bear to see the word Gestapo typed out. I translate and retranslate, hoping there's been a mistake, but the letters are insistent—they keep saying the same thing. I claw through another spill of ugly tears. The coffee grows stale beside me. I understand that I have no right to be sad about this. I have not earned it. I did not have to pay.

It is true that scholars disagree on how much we can trust what is written in the NKVD criminal files. As the Soviets reclaimed these territories, the immediate postwar trials were rushed, politicized events and revenge the mood of the hour. One historian argues that *patterns* of behavior might be inferred from a collection of case files, though it is difficult to confirm the details of individual cases. It is possible an official was given orders to fabricate Joseph's crimes and not one single word of this NKVD report is accurate. It is possible I am the worst sort of snake for speaking about that which we cannot verify. Perhaps I am perpetuating the same falsehoods as the Soviet regime, albeit for different reasons. Maybe RT (Russia Today) will excerpt my words and use them in the Kremlin's wartime propaganda campaign to demonize Ukrainians, *Banderovtsy, Banderovtsy, Banderovtsy* . . . Can you trust the archivist of your enemy? Perhaps only as much, or as little, as you trust your own desperate, wolfish memory. Whether Joseph was directly responsible for those seven or not, seven people, somewhere, were killed by Gestapo. Our family of seven was spared, at least temporarily. Theirs was not. I am alive, which is the only fact I can trust.

My great-grandfather was one of 320,000 Soviet citizens arrested after the war for suspected German collaboration. He was found guilty under article 54-1a, betrayal of the Motherland. It did not matter, of course, that Joseph and his family had only been Soviet citizens for a little over one year, prior to the four years of Nazi occupation. It did not matter that the Soviets had oppressed and starved Ukrainians and that Joseph wanted nothing to do with Stalin or his stupid empire. How can you betray those to which you have no loyalty? It also did not matter that the Soviets and the Germans had carved up the bloodlands among themselves and in 1939 signed the Molotov-Ribbentrop agreement, a secret non-aggression pact that started WWII in the first place. That the Soviets had—on a grand and disastrous scale—collaborated with the Nazis. Had the Germans not reneged and pushed into the Eastern territories, the Soviets would have no doubt remained their allies. But these sweeping historical circumstances did not matter, and Joseph was shipped to Siberia for betrayal.

I read later that if you or a close family member had ever exhibited loyalty to the communist party, your sentence might have been made more lenient. I suspect from how Busia spoke about the Bolsheviks that her father was not granted any leniency. He was accused of shipping people in a cattle car to faraway Germany. He himself was shipped in a cattle car to faraway Siberia. There is a sort of gross equilibrium in the punishment, as if, together, suffering and oppression form a cyclic machine. We are each a cog, though we tend to forget this—I forget this. I am a tooth on a wheel that's been spinning for decades.

My foray into these papers yields another bit of information, news to me, a family secret tucked neatly under the shirt collar of *I not remember*. Busia's brother Ivan was arrested by the NKVD in 1940, during that single year of Soviet rule, that one very long and very short year before the Germans arrived. It does not say what he was accused of, though from what I knew of him as an adult, it was likely on account of some anti-Bolshevik activity. Ivan was an outspoken Ukrainian patriot. Knock, knock, and a smell like almonds. And so, at the age of 19, he was arrested and jailed in nearby Dubno for 7 months. They released him eventually, citing a lack of adequate grounds on which to build a case. Had he not been released exactly then, Uncle Ivan would have likely been massacred alongside the rest of the 550 inmates in Dubno prison when the Soviets withdrew in 1941. The retreating army didn't want to leave behind any enemies for the Germans to use. I learned, too, from these papers that Joseph's patronymic name was Ivanovich. He had named his son after his own father.

Busia's brother Ivan had a very handsome smile, and when I was a child, he would always tuck a five-dollar bill into my hand on his way out the door. Abraham Lincoln's prominent jaw matched his own. I was 11 when Uncle Ivan died, and I remember it being the first time I cried over a dead person.

I read elsewhere that recently, in 2017, a ledger was found inside a buried milk churn in western Ukraine. It listed the names of people from my family's region who were taken by the Soviets. It was a known partisan tactic—hiding important information in milk cans—and so the authorities began numbering and dating each can issued. If a milk cooperative could not produce the correct number of cans, someone was suspected of underground activity. Was Ivan's name in that milk churn? Was his father's? It is reported that a small *samizdat* pamphlet called "Instructions for Parents in Upbringing Children" was also stuck inside the churn. The pamphlet was printed in 1950 with the aim of helping Ukrainians resist Bolshevik rule, but as I read the first instruction ("Explain to children that Russians are not our older brothers"), a hundred headlines from the current war shoot through my brain.

UKRAINE AND RUSSIA'S SIBLING RIVALRY.

RUSSIA VS. UKRAINE: A CLASH OF BROTHERS, NOT
CULTURES.
PUTIN TREATING UKRAINE LIKE A BROTHER?

It seems very little has changed, and I am struck by our impulse
to claim family, no matter how cruel we are to them. Am I cruel
for entertaining these possibilities about my family, its members long-gone, unable to provide their own defense? Maybe
Czesław Miłosz was right: When a writer is born into a family,
the family is finished.

The archive documents create more blanks than they fill.
The NKVD papers do not tell me how much Busia and her siblings knew, or how they felt about what their father may have
been doing during the war. All over their region, Jews were
being targeted, their homes and possessions seized, ghet-
tos created and then liquidated, bodies discarded in pits. Jewish villagers were hiding in forests all around them, and so my
grandmother's family must have known what was happening.
The NKVD documents, however, do not allude to the mass
murder of Jews at all. It is well understood now that after the
war the Soviet government tended to downplay the Holocaust
as a specifically Jewish tragedy, and the USSR's closed borders
did not allow for exposure to the reckoning process that had
begun in the West. Instead, the Soviet regime co-opted Jewish
WWII suffering for its own agenda, often labeling the victims
simply "Soviet citizens." I guess distant victimhood is an easy
shroud to reach for.

The scans I received from the archive are yellow and brittle-
looking. Between the short phrases scrawled in pencil, there
are lines and lines of blank tan, a constellation of blank spaces,
like so many sprawling wheat fields. There are empty fields
where there should be people.

A few kilometers down the road from the village, there is
an unmarked mass grave, which I learn about from a Jewish

database online. It's along the same road Busia and her sisters walked on their way to town, where they went to buy sugar and *vyshyvanka* thread. Today, the hill of bones is tucked behind a cement gas station. I've driven by several times and never knew to stop.

As I scroll through the trial documents, the hiccup settles into my gut. It is heavy as guilt. My mind wanders to South Dakota and to the Catholic school classroom where I first heard of Babyn Yar. The priests there would so often speak about *original sin,* and for the first time, I think I know what they mean, how we are a crowd condemned. Seven people whose names I don't know were killed by Gestapo, and we are accused of being an accessory. I am the reason there is a man slouching dead on the cross. This is an interesting difference between the Orthodox and the Catholics, the church of the East and the church of the West. In the Orthodox tradition, they say we have inherited from Adam and Eve a condition of sin, which is death. In the Catholic tradition, they say we have inherited both the condition of sin and its guilt. To be alive, then, is to be guilty. I was raised on little hot sauce packets from Taco Bell, and I was raised on guilt, and this must be why I have decided to leaf through the archive papers, to look down into the ravine where we try not to look. *Holy God, Holy Mighty, Holy Immortal, have mercy on us. Have mercy on us. Have mercy.*

The records show that Joseph's wife and children were not in the back field riding horses, or down in the cellar, or tending potatoes at the time of his arrest, as I had always thought. They were already in Germany. This does not make sense. Hadn't Busia told me about the bad men coming to the door? Their incessant knocking? Those Moskali bastards with their Bolshevik atheism and their Russian imperialism? Hadn't she told me about *them?* Surely, the day of Joseph's arrest that plays on foggy loop in my mind is a day constructed from fact. How could I have gotten it so wrong? Do I remember Busia saying it specifically—*bad men, knock, knock?* Am I recalling the last time I recalled it? Did Busia mine from her own memory, or from someone else's? Am I just a reflection of a reflection?

At the time of his arrest, Joseph's wife and children were already serving as *ostarbeiters,* as slave laborers in another country's economy. According to the documents, Joseph was accused of coordinating three shipments of Ukrainian villagers to serve as *ostarbeiters*—

> Knock, knock. 50 inhabitants.
> Busia is raising someone else's babies.
> Knock, knock. 46.
> Children teaching you the enemy tongue.
> Knock, knock. 55.
> A scrap of bone caught in our throat, like swallowing glass.

—And suddenly I am worried it was never about whistling inside the house, or Chicagoland news, or even only about Stalin's secret police. There was no more dangerous place in the world than Ukraine, but perhaps the thing we are most afraid of followed us home. It glares from the mirror in the kitchen. Faced with impossible choices, we, too, could be made accessories in some terror.

What I mean is: the thing we are most afraid of is ourself.

+++

Above my writing desk in this American blue state there is another mirror. I did not put it there. It was placed on the wall by my landlord. You can tell I had nothing to do with this mirror because it is far too high for me. I must strain on dagger toes to see the top half of my face and the single gray strand mushrooming up from my part. In this sense, it is not a very useful mirror. It is, at least, not very useful for spotting the dill between your incisor and your canine on the left side. *Ty ho-lodna yak volk?* Hungry as a wolf, you think, picking the green from your mouth. No, this mirror hangs instead like a hidden portrait. Like a mug shot you've tried

and tried
and tried to bury.

The mirror is too high, but after translating the archive documents, I stretch to see myself in it. My hair is greasy. My forehead pores gape, each one a small ravine, full of things invisible to me. Why did this face, this terribly average face, emerge from the war? Why us? Why *me?* In that moment, I am an impossible woman with impossible questions. Later, I will read Gitta Sereny's interview with Franz Stangl, the SS commandant of Treblinka and Sobibór. He is sitting in prison after being found guilty for the murders of 900,000 people. "My guilt," he says, "is that I am still here."

I am nothing like Franz Stangl. I have not murdered one single person, but when he says this, I feel almost as if I understand him. There is something vaguely criminal about just being alive. It is an awful responsibility, so easily abused. Certainly for me, it is a harrowing privilege, when seven lived and seven died. I have not yet read about Franz Stangl, but as I am stretching to see my face in the mirror that morning, I already know my guilt: I am still here.

And if you are wondering about your own guilt, find a reflective surface. There are many options for this. A glass storefront. A black lake. A stork's egg, a sunflower, a snake. Any object angled toward the future should do. Now, hold it up to your face, approximately six inches away. At this point the answer is simple. It is the feel of your teeth.

I SAW THE SUNSHINE, MELTING

[Chernobyl] was perhaps the real cause
of the collapse of the Soviet Union.

—Mikhail Gorbachev

We lost a family member to Chernobyl. Lost is not a euphemism.

My beloved great aunt Nadia was married to my great uncle Vasyl, and Vasyl's younger cousin is the one we lost. I never met this cousin, and I don't know his name. So, I lost my great uncle's no-name cousin to Chernobyl.

It's worth noting here that when my Ukrainian family talks about *family* they don't always mean in the nuclear sense. I learned from an early age that if a distant relative needs help, you should write them a check, even if you've never met before. Phone calls to relatives are mandatory on birthdays, anniversaries, death day anniversaries, and certain name days, regardless of how young you are. Such familial duty is, in a way, oddly liberating. It leaves little to whim or affection or bothersome detail like geography. In this, our Ukrainian-Chicago sense of family, blood (or blood-by-marriage) is the only prerequisite for belonging.

So, I lost a family member to Chernobyl. In 1986 he was a bus driver in Kyiv. Post-Soviet capitals like Kyiv boast an impressive array of public transportation options. There are taxis, trains, trams, subways, city buses, regional buses, and minibuses that act like big-group shared taxis and will pick you up anywhere you can hail one. These taxi-buses are called *marshrutky*, and they are usually painted a scorching, screaming shade of yellow. After the collapse of the USSR and the introduction of the market economy, entrepreneurs emerged from every floor of every apartment block. A savvy entrepreneur could buy one of these golden taxi-buses for 8,000 US dollars and have it paid off within a year. They called this period in the 1990s the Marshrutka Boom. Driving professionally both before and after the collapse, my great uncle's no-name cousin was a *marshrutka* driver.

The accident at the Vladimir Ilyich Lenin Nuclear Power Plant in Chernobyl happened in the middle of the night. Twelve hours after dual explosions melted the core of Reactor 4, residents of the nearby factory town of Prypiat were swimming, playing soccer, and fishing from the stream that feeds into the plant's cooling reservoir. It wasn't until the following day that the announcement was made: *Vnimaniye, vnimaniye! . . . radioactive conditions in the vicinity are deteriorating . . . children being top priority . . . each apartment block will have a bus at its disposal . . . it is highly advisable to take your documents . . .*

The drive from Kyiv to Prypiat is two and half hours. The accident happened on a holiday weekend, right before the annual May Day parade—what the Soviets called the "Day of International Workers' Solidarity"—when many Kyiv-based *marshrutka* drivers were supposed to have time off. Instead 1,200 drivers were called up for an unusual assignment: drive north to the factory town, pick up as many people as you can, and make sure they don't bring too much luggage. My great uncle's no-name cousin was one of these 1,200 burnt-yellow bus drivers, sitting in a line of traffic that stretched for miles and hours. The images from that Sunday are beautiful. The sky that weekend was pure blue, the buildings gray and square, the trees a blooming springtime green, and the road was a river of butter, inching lazily into the heart of the town and then away from it. I read one account in which a resident of Prypiat, who was a child at the time, said she doesn't remember the accident at all, only the buses. Another resident later described the buses as a parade of giant beetles. I imagine them more as a procession of creeping suns, each responsible for a whole, tiny world.

One might assume that a scene like this would incite panic, but from what I've heard and read, that was not entirely the case. Residents were told that the evacuation was temporary, that they'd be allowed to return soon. No reports were made regarding the long-term physical dangers of radiation exposure. The bus drivers, for example, were told nothing about safety. There is one story passed through my family in low whispers. No one likes to talk about this cousin anymore because he can't be easily helped. The story carries a trace of black comedy, as if it were an inappropriate joke: When traffic was at a standstill that Sunday April 27th, my great uncle's no-name cousin and some of the other drivers got out of their vehicles, took off their shirts, and sunbathed by the stream. It was a holiday weekend, after all, so they lazed around for the afternoon, bare-chested and beaming. They were told nothing.

I'm not sure how many looping trips back and forth to Prypiat my relative made in those days after the accident. Maybe just one, maybe fifteen. I do know that shortly thereafter he started to drink more and developed health problems. Perhaps, like other drivers, his eyesight failed or his teeth fell out. His alcohol abuse became so excessive that my family in the States lost contact with him. We tried and couldn't get ahold of him, didn't know where he went, didn't know what happened. We lost him. My great aunt Nadia and her husband Vasyl both died a few years ago, and maybe our no-name cousin is dead, too. The official Soviet death toll counted only 31 from the accident itself. But today, if they accounted for all the premature deaths—the leukemia, thyroid cancer, suicide—that number would be in the thousands, though it's hard to measure with exactitude a thing that kills so insidiously. I don't know what happened to my no-name cousin, but I do know that very few of those Chernobyl bus drivers are still alive.

As for the fate of the buses, that, too, is unclear. In between trips to Prypiat they were hosed down in an attempt to wash away any dangerous elements before hauling the next load of passengers, before uprooting another small collection of lives. After several weeks of ongoing evacuations, I suspect authorities ordered the destruction of the buses, though I have no evidence to prove it. I hope someone mandated the burial of those tiny, glowing stars, those giant beetles. But truthfully, I wouldn't be surprised to learn that the Chernobyl *marshrutky* were still on the road somewhere, driving in sluggish circles, revolving.

These yellow minibuses that evacuated the town of Prypiat were all identical, manufactured by a bus company based in Budapest that, during the 1970s and 80s, supplied the Soviet Union with something like 12,000 buses annually. This Hungarian company is called Ikarus (or, Icarus), and the bus is the Ikarus Z60, its logo a set of sleek wings. I've lost the name of my cousin, and so this Ikarus name is all I have to replace it. Its three syllables sound like dark humor, like a looping joke you can't escape, this name both warning and reminder: A warning that when we mix our science and our hubris, we risk flying too close to the sun. And a reminder of our melting.

+++

It's worth noting here that Ukrainian-Americans in general and Chicago-Ukrainians specifically tend to be quite vocal about issues of lineage. From a very young age, I could name a slew of celebrities with Ukrainian roots: Mila Kunis, Larisa Oleynik, Jack Palance (a distant relative, I'm told), Vera Farmiga, Mike

Ditka, Chuck Palahniuk (another rumored relative), Alex Trebek. Even today it's rare for me to be somewhere when *Jeopardy!* comes on the television and not announce to the entire room that *vin nash*—he's one of ours. Because Ukrainian language, culture, and identity were so demonized by our old country occupiers (the Poles, the Germans, and the Soviets), when our families arrived in North America, the first impulse was to proclaim and reclaim what had been denied. We felt entitled to name things and people as ours.

And it was this milieu of dogged reclamation that engendered in me a kind of latent nationalism, pride for a place I had never even been. It was this milieu that resulted in me, an obnoxious seventh-grade know-it-all in South Dakota, waving my hand during science class to inform my teacher that our textbook was misleading, that the world's worst nuclear disaster had not just happened in *the USSR* but rather that it had happened in *Ukraine,* which is now a sovereign nation, not at all Soviet, and not at all Russian. And, while we're on the subject, a sovereign nation called simply *Ukraine.* Not *the* Ukraine.

I felt compelled to tell my science teacher and my classmates (who were busy daydreaming about what to order at Taco Bell after school, and who surely couldn't care less) that the plant had been in Ukraine, that the suffering was *ours.* Technically, my announcement wasn't wrong, but it was, I see now, a sign of how preciously we hold our victimhood. I was not around for the purges or the famine; I was raised on little hot sauce packets. Mine was a split family with homes in different states; I was never *taken away* like my relatives were. And yet, I had still inherited a sense of victimhood. There I was, a tiny patriot-in-training, using our people's historical traumas to justify why my surname stuck out among my peers, to justify why I had to leave each summer and live with my foreign grandmother. If I was going to be made to feel strange by the everyday interrogations—*Wow, how long did it take you to learn how to spell that?*— then I should at least be allowed to claim some big excitement. And I could think of nothing more exciting than the world's worst nuclear disaster. Distant victimhood is an easy shroud to reach for.

But, if I had really known what I was talking about then, I would have also told my science teacher that the wind was blowing north that day. I would have told her that 70% of the Chernobyl fallout floated into what is now Belarus and that several million Belarusians still live on contaminated land. I would have said that this is especially important because for the past 25 years, Belarus has been ruled by a dictator who is desperate to rehabilitate the nuclear ideal. A dictator with a nasty habit of silencing dissent. Alexander Lukashenko is a Belarusian dictator with a Ukrainian grandfather and a Ukrainian last name, though I may not have been so eager to tell my teacher that part.

+++

In 2011 I moved to Belarus on a Fulbright grant, though truthfully, I knew little about the place save for its geographic and cultural proximity to Ukraine. Before moving, I read whatever I could find about the country in English (which wasn't much), and noticed an obvious, recurring theme: Chernobyl. Though the disaster was mentioned in every book and article, the threat of lingering radiation seemed negligible. Most sources indicated that, for a temporary resident of Minsk, as I was to be, the risks were minimal. They did discourage drinking tap water and consuming local dairy products, particularly in the south; they said to avoid forest fruits and wild mushrooms, which are notorious for soaking up radioactivity. But beyond these few mild suggestions, little noise was made about any present-day danger. I was undeterred by the idea of Chernobyl and its forbidden fruit. If anything, I was vaguely compelled by it. This is, of course, the gross privilege of a western traveler: I was inclined to romanticize the dictators and disasters of other places, almost as if they existed for the purpose of adding texture to whatever adventure I was writing for myself. Why else was I attracted to contamination? To corruption?

While English-language sources were quick to associate Chernobyl with Belarus, I lived in the capital city for just under one year and didn't hear much about it. Chernobyl wasn't a daily topic of conversation, though it did come up occasionally. I remember sitting with a friend on a bench outside the university where we both worked. She was waiting to go to a gynecologist appointment and when I asked if everything was okay, she told me that it was normal for women in Belarus to go twice a year, that it was encouraged. *The air is bad here—from Chernobyl,* she said nonchalantly, as if that explained everything. Another time one of my co-workers told me about a brilliant pianist she knew of. According to her story, the pianist's wrist bones had become very frail and would break whenever she tried to play the piano. She would be playing *Moonlight Sonata* or some classical tune, and her bones would crumble like cookies. My co-worker said that *of course it was just radiation.* This is how Chernobyl would sneak into conversation: casually, matter-of-factly.

For Belarusians, the world's worst nuclear disaster had been sapped of its drama. It was just another environmental circumstance, like how Minnesotans expect snow and Floridians are accustomed to humidity or the yearly hurricane. Sure, it was unpleasant and would sometimes cause bad things to happen, but mostly it was a plain fact of life. My Belarusian friends waited on benches before doctor appointments, as I fought the impulse to sensationalize their lives.

In Minsk I made friends with a local college student named Anya. She was shockingly tall and slender, with thick, shiny hair that fell to her lower back, and the build of a ballerina. She was teaching herself English and studying Tourism & Hospitality. She wanted to leave Belarus. In a few years, Anya would find a job on a cruise ship and post photos from every continent, her ballerina body bikini-clad on beaches of searing blue. But, for now, Anya was still landlocked. She had never left Belarus save for trips to Russia and Ukraine, which, according to her, *don't really count*. For now, Anya lived vicariously through the foreigners who passed through town.

It was April when Anya invited me to dinner at her family's home where she lived with her parents and sister. I took the metro out to one of the farthest stations and emerged from the underground to a cluster of gray Soviet tower block apartments. Anya's neighborhood looked like most Belarusian suburbs. Inside her family's flat, it was clear that Anya and her mother had been cooking all day for me, the foreigner. The table's spread was imposing with upwards of 10 different dishes, Russian champagne, fine crystal, and an intricately embroidered tablecloth. It looked too lovely to eat.

After several minutes of fawning over the table, Anya, her mother, and I began sampling dishes and chatting in our part-English, part-Russian. Anya's father was there, too, but as we ate, I noticed he wasn't touching the food. Anya must have noticed me noticing because she said that her father's stomach was bothering him today, as it often did. She went on to explain that her father had been a Chernobyl liquidator and that for five months after the accident he had served in the exclusion zone as part of a government cleanup crew. I stopped mid-bite. It felt rude to enjoy potato pancakes and pineapple-chicken salad in front of him.

Why? I asked, not exactly sure what I was asking. In general, Anya's father had a very serious, even grim-looking face, but at my question it cracked a little. He smirked at my naïveté, at my foreignness.

I had no choice, he said. *They made us.*

He then stood up and took a medal out of a nearby cabinet and handed it to me. It was a medal of honor, issued by the Soviets, for his liquidation work. The medal had the Greek letters for alpha, beta, and gamma—three types of radiation—suspended over a drop of blood. The background was bright blue.

Father has a lot of health problems, mostly in his stomach, Anya said to me, in English. *But because of his status we're higher up on the list to get a new flat from the government.* When she said this, her voice didn't sound hopeful. This was, after all, 26 years after the accident. *Probably Lukashenko will cut these benefits soon anyways,* she sighed. Though I wanted to ask more questions about this, I could tell the family was not interested in further articulating these gloomier bits of reality lurking below their perfectly laid table. Their reluctance reminded me of my Ukrainian family, our impulse to point loud fingers at Alex Trebek while speaking in hushed tones about our own cousins. Some things are easier to name than others.

Rather than dwell on her husband's health issues, Anya's mother briskly changed the subject and began telling me in Russian about how she won the English Olympiad back when she was in school. She loved English class, she said, and she had been the best at it. She could even recall her favorite line from an English poem that her teacher had made them memorize decades ago.

I saw the sunshine in the blue sky, she half-squealed, in a thick Russian accent. *I saw the sunshine in the blue sky, oh my!* Anya's mother laughed hysterically, as if tickled by the sound of her own voice.

That's really great, I said. *Do you know any more lines?*

I saw the sunshine in the blue sky. I saw the sunshine in the blue sky, oh my!

No, Mama, Anya said in Russian. *She wants to know if you remember the rest.*

I saw the sunshine in the blue sky, her mother replied in English before switching to Russian. *No, that's all. It is so nice to have an American to listen, isn't it?*

I nodded and said something about how impressive her memory was. She smiled at me, taking a small sip from her flute. Over the course of our dinner, Anya's mother proudly delivered her line—*I saw the sunshine in the blue sky, oh my, oh my!*—at least a dozen times.

After dessert and more champagne, I began to feel sleepy. I offered to help clean up, but Belarusian superstition wouldn't allow it. *Do you want us to have bad luck forever?* Anya asked. As I put on my scarf to leave and take the metro back downtown, Anya's father pulled something else out of the glass cabinet. He handed me a heavy silver coin. It was worth one ruble and had Lenin's profile on the front. On the back were the hammer and sickle, the USSR's state emblem, and a commemoration: "One Hundred Years Since the Birthday of V. I. Lenin, 1870–1970." I held the coin delicately and looked at Anya.

What's this for? I asked. She turned to her father.

You can keep it, he said in Russian. *I know foreigners always love this Soviet stuff.* At this Anya and her parents laughed. It was a kind-of joke, but at whose expense I'm not sure. Mine maybe? Theirs? Lenin's? Anya's father was right. I was a foreigner who loved collecting Soviet kitsch. Several months earlier, when I met Anya's grandmother, she had gifted me an ashtray commemorating the 40th anniversary of the October Revolution. When I protested that it must be old and valuable and sentimental and that she should keep it, Anya's grandmother said pointedly, *We don't care about that crap anymore.*

So I nodded and thanked Anya's father and descended back into Minsk's shallow metro system. I admired the intricate tiles on the floor of the train tunnel while rubbing the silver coin inside my purse. Today, over seven years since that dinner, I still keep the Lenin coin in my purse. It has moved to three countries with me and passed through many more states; it has been on every trip to the post office and grocery store. It's a heavy coin, and I like to feel its thick edge when I reach inside my purse for a pen. I'm glad when I remember that it's there, quietly serving as some sort of strange luck charm. And the Lenin coin is itself a reminder: of Anya's grandmother, her swollen legs rocking to the pulse of the television, a garish Russian variety show. Of Anya's father, slouching, his chair pushed back from the table, barely enough to notice. Of Anya's mother, distracting us with her blue sky and her sunshine. Of Anya, this child of Belarus, poised for flight.

Is it also a warning, this Lenin-faced coin? Sometimes I stand it on edge and roll it across the hardwood floor. It spins round and around, as if it will go forever.

+++

The only other sustained conversation about Chernobyl I can remember from that year in Minsk was one I had with a co-worker named Sveta. It was her birthday and we were having coffee at some café in the center of town. I don't recall now how it came up, but I probably asked where she was from. Sveta said she was born in Gomel, in the far southeast of Belarus, but left there at a young age. Gomel region sits just north of Prypiat and shares a long border with Ukraine. Because of the northerly wind that day in April 1986, Gomel got the brunt of the fallout. Chernobyl happened when Sveta was two years old and her parents, concerned for her health, sent her to live with relatives in Moscow for a while.

I'm not sure what Sveta's parents did for a living, but, unlike many, they had the means to leave. After Sveta's stint in Moscow, the whole family resettled to Smorgon, a small town in the northwest corner of Belarus, about as far away from the station, and the fallout, and the glowing mushrooms as they could get without emigrating. Smorgon, then, is where Sveta spent most of her youth. As she's telling me this over the steam of coffee, I notice her blue eyes turn both dreamy and alarmed-looking, like she, too, has left the stove on somewhere. Sveta smirks, even laughs a bit before saying, *And now Smorgon is where Lukashenko has decided to build Belarus's first nuclear plant.* She pauses, digesting her own words. *It's ironic, yes?*

In 2002 Lukashenko stated that he was against the construction of a nuclear facility on the territory of Belarus. But, in 2007, after an energy dispute between Belarus and Russia—who supplies most of its neighbors with energy and routinely uses price hikes as a political tool—Lukashenko changed his tune. He is quoted saying that a domestic energy source is an issue of "national security," and given that Russia is the sole supplier of gas to Belarus, he's not wrong. The country would do well to diversify its energy supply.

But Lukashenko's executive decision to build a nuclear plant a mere 50 kilometers from Sveta's home in Smorgon is steeped in even more irony than she expressed that day in the café. Because Belarus can't afford the project on its own, it has taken out a nine billion dollar loan from the Russian government. It was also decided in 2009 that a Russian company would build the plant. The first reactor vessel, weighing over 700,000 pounds, was delivered by train to the construction site in February 2016. It was built by a Russian manufacturer.

The new Astravets Nuclear Power Plant, as it's called, has not gone unprotested. Belarusian groups have campaigned against Russian involvement in the project while others have objected to the use of any and all nuclear energy on the territory of Belarus. Every year on April 26th there is a Chernobyl anniversary rally in Minsk and at these demonstrations people loudly voice opposition to the Astravets project. Most years, the Chernobyl anniversary rally ends with police intervention, the detention of protestors and journalists, and zero media coverage on state-owned TV channels.

State media instead shows only government-sanctioned Chernobyl meetings and memorials. For example, in 2011 on the eve of the anniversary, a group of liquidators was invited to meet with parliamentarians at the House of Representatives. The liquidators gathered in a conference room, wore mostly blue suits with striped ties, their hair all gray and white and sharply cut. They sat on plush seats and were each handed an enormous bouquet of red flowers, roses so big and red they didn't look real. Government officials spoke into microphones and said things like *altruism, bravery, professionalism.* They said things like *fight for normalcy, ensure public order.* One firefighter was invited to tell his story from that day at the plant. He explained how his crew was on the roof of the station for 90 minutes before they started fainting. *Many of those who worked alongside me died a painful death,* the liquidator said. *Their skin turned black.*

The last to speak was Anatoly Rubinov, the parliament's Chairman of the Council. *Chernobyl should not become a black mark on the path of modern day energy development in Belarus,* he said into the microphone. *The twenty-five-year-old tragedy must not influence our decision to build our own nuclear power station.* Rubinov concluded the meeting by thanking the liquidators and reiterating that they deserve the utmost respect for their work. Camera and film crews lined the perimeter of the wood-paneled room. From these official photos, you can see the liquidators' eyes, all blue and shining.

+++

That same year, just six months after the meeting with Rubinov and seven after Japan's Fukushima nuclear disaster, liquidators in Ukraine were protesting. Nearly a thousand people, liquidators and family members, gathered on November 1st outside the Ukrainian parliament in Kyiv to express their anger at a proposed bill that would cut their benefits. There is a black metal gate and a line of Berkut special forces officers standing between the liquidators and the parliament building. *Shame! Shame! Shame!* the protestors chant as they break down the gate, wrestle with the men in blue camouflage uniforms, and eventually flood the steps of parliament. One liquidator is interviewed from the crowd. *I came because I don't have anything to buy medicine with,* he says. *We'll take parliament down brick by brick. And hang the MPs one by one.*

While liquidators were promised reasonable benefits immediately after their service—subsidized medical care, university admission, a guaranteed pension, sanatorium privileges, etc.—many of these have since been eliminated or drastically reduced. Today, most liquidators residing in Ukraine, Belarus, and Russia receive between 100 and 200 USD a month, a paltry sum in the face of chronic health problems. And, like Anya's father, most were never granted the adequate housing they were once promised. The more than 700,000 liquidators who served in the months after the Chernobyl accident helped spare Europe from excessive radioactive fallout. But in recent years, it has not been uncommon for those same liquidators to stage protests and pursue legal action in the struggle for some kind of just compensation.

A few weeks after protestors stormed the parliament building in Kyiv, a group of 40 liquidators in the eastern Ukrainian city of Donetsk, the heart of the Donbass region, declared a hunger strike and pitched tents outside the pension funds building. The men gathered around makeshift fire pits for warmth and tied white bandages to their foreheads, the words Я ГОЛОДАЮ—I'm starving—written in careful letters across the front. Several weeks into the demonstration, a midnight skirmish erupts as Donetsk police officers attempt to forcibly dismantle the tent city. It's been 25 years since the accident and Ukrainian authorities have lost their patience, are tired of providing for these veterans; by now, they hope people have forgotten, or have chosen to forget. We don't have time to be reminded of this failure in vision. We don't have time to interrogate old ideology when everyone is starving. We don't have time for this. We're tired.

During the midnight altercation one man, Gennady Konoplyov, who had been complaining earlier of chest pains, is shoved by police and dies on his way to the hospital. Two days later, the liquidators carry an empty, burgundy-draped coffin through the streets, a symbolic funeral for the 70-year-old whose thick, white hair once stood straight up like grass from his protest bandage. *I'm starving.* The casket thudding hollow as the pallbearers' stomachs.

It is winter, and while the liquidators march with Gennady's coffin they are bundled from head to toe in dark, heavy clothes. They wear only grays, browns, black. Some women walk alongside, dabbing their faces with handkerchiefs. Others carry glowing red votive candles. The mourners inch slowly in this most solemn of parades, the backs of their worn leather overcoats shining in the frozen light. Shining, I suppose, like a line of beetles.

+++

Every year at Christmastime, my Chicago-Ukrainian family takes up a collection. I write a check to Marina and Yarosh. Though I have met these cousins several times, most of my relatives who contribute to the annual Christmas fund never have. We are decades and oceans away from the old country and the accident, but duty is a feeling we still can't shake.

When Belarusian writer Svetlana Alexievich won the Nobel Prize in 2015, I took it as an opportunity to reread her book

Voices from Chernobyl: The Oral History of a Nuclear Disaster. In it there is a monologue by a woman named Lyudmila Polenkaya, a village teacher who was evacuated from the exclusion zone. She talks about the holiday celebrations that week after the accident in 1986. "We all dressed up our kids and took them to the May Day demonstration," she says. "We could go or not go, as we pleased. No one forced us to go, or demanded that we go. But we thought it was our duty. Of course! At such a time, on such a day—everyone should be together. We ran along the streets, in the crowd."

Lyudmila goes on to tell how she remembers seeing the secretaries of the regional Party committee there at the parade. She remembers the young daughter of the first secretary, how the girl was standing up for people to see. The secretary's daughter was wearing a raincoat and hat, even though it was sunny out. This is very important to Lyudmila—that the children of Party leaders were there that May Day, beaming in the bright open air. She concludes her reflection: "It's not just the land that's contaminated, but our minds."

Why am I drawn to contamination? To corruption? Maybe this sense of duty to the fatherland is an inherited thing. Maybe writing a check to a stranger is like writing a story about a stranger is like driving a bus full of strangers. Of course, I know, this is a conflation of things that should never be conflated. Who am I to sketch such crude comparisons, after all? Who am I to scream into the frozen light that *vin nash*—he is ours?

+++

There is another story (or perhaps a joke) about a man with no name. It is Saturday morning, it is springtime. He is shirtless, working in the yard of his modest village home. Sunrays on his skin feel so pleasant after the long, lonely winter. He is outside for just 15 minutes, but his chest and arms have already bronzed. The man, both pleased and puzzled, runs inside the house to show his wife what a beautiful tan he's acquired in so little time, oh my! Fifteen minutes later, he is vomiting.

Acute radiation syndrome is first marked by nausea and dizziness. The worst of the skin burns don't develop until later. They are more like boils really, like your skin is boiling, like there are volcanoes swelling from your skin. They are a grove of secrets mushrooming up and out toward the light. They crack into so many different colors. There are rainbow-stained volcanoes all over your chest and arms. You stepped outside to feed the chickens and to survey the apple blossoms and now your body is melting from the inside out. Your body is a meltdown.

At what was once the Vladimir Ilyich Lenin Nuclear Power Plant in Chernobyl, the infamous Reactor 4 is shrouded in a concrete sarcophagus. According to experts, the Soviet-era containment structure is leaking and badly in need of replacement. They've been working on that, making a new tomb with international funds. This New Safe Confinement arch was constructed just a few hundred meters away from the Reactor. At the end of 2016, they moved the 850-foot-wide, 35,000-ton arch along a Teflon-coated track and secured it atop the plant, earning it the distinction of the world's largest manmade object to ever move on land. It was made to withstand tornadoes and earthquakes and is expected to last for 100 years. The new tomb rises high above the gray apartment blocs and irrepressible green of Prypiat. From faraway, the shiny arch looks more like a modern concert venue or event stage, a place to gather for Independence Day shows, than it does a nuclear coffer. It is an unexpected thing to celebrate.

But beneath the old sarcophagus and inside the core of Reactor 4, there remains a black, molten mass. It is lava formed into rings like the loops of a tree. I am told that the molten mass is burning—that it is still on fire—but this is a difficult thing to confirm. Who wants to look down there? I am also told that the Ukrainian government has announced plans to turn the exclusion zone into a solar energy farm. They will fill 5,000 acres with solar panels, they will turn the field into a dish rack, each plate tilted at 30 degrees. We will leverage the mean sun! they say. We will make lemonade! they say. But, of course, workers must be careful not to disturb the dirt around the panels.

Over thirty years later, the wolves and deer have returned. The wild boars are back. Prezwalski's horse is here. People are relocating to the exclusion zone from Donbass. "Radiation may kill us slowly," one settler said, "but it doesn't shoot or bomb us." The Presidents with their Ukrainian names are giving speeches in front of the sarcophagus, and the sun is shining, what a beautiful day. A beautiful day, the sun is scorching, it is burning money! The wolves have returned and the mushrooms are scraping their fresh caps against the sky, oh my, oh my! And the core is still melting.

My family would rather I stop talking about our no-name cousin out there somewhere, melting from the inside. We can't help him anymore, and this depresses us. As Americans, we like to accomplish things—make phone calls, write checks—and then move on with our day. We don't have time to wallow over old ideology. We don't have time to be reminded.

But I am stubborn. I want to find my no-name cousin. I want to find him, and fill his belly with potato pancakes and sautéed onions. I want to place cold washcloths on his swollen skin. I want to look him in the rainbow-stained eyes and call him family. Soon, on our way to the revolution, we will learn each other's names.

THE VILLAGE (DA CAPO)

On the day we go to the village, I know many things. I know, for example, that Bohdan will be punctual, arriving at 6:55am to escort us once again in his Mercedes van, northward from Lviv. I know we will stop for another *fotosessiya* in a field of flowers, though the poppies are probably wilted by now. It is sunflower season. I know Bohdan and Chris will want to share music and that I will help translate what falls outside the notes. It will not always be a good translation—my grammar is bad, I've forgotten many words while in America—but it is my best attempt at something musical. When I am self-deprecating about how my Ukrainian is deteriorating, Bohdan will agree with me. *Yes. Yes, it is.*

I know that the day we return to the village, July 19, 2018, is also the 67th day of Oleg Sentsov's hunger strike. Sentsov, a Ukrainian filmmaker, was arrested in his native Crimea back in May 2014, a few months after Russia annexed the peninsula and while I was still living in Lviv. Sentsov was active on Maidan, and he vocally opposed Russia's annexation of his home region. The authorities accused him, among other things, of plotting to blow up a Lenin statue in Simferopol. He claims false witness testimonies were secured using torture, and that his interrogators threatened to sexually assault him. A Moscow court denied Sentsov his Ukrainian citizenship. Although we have only a river and no sea to speak of, Crimea is not so unlike the village: one day, you may wake up in a new empire. Sentsov was sentenced to 20 years in a Siberian prison camp.

As our van floats through Lviv in the gray morning light, Oleg Sentsov's name is strung around the city like a curtain. He has demanded the release of all Ukrainian political prisoners held in Russia and won't eat until then. So, Sentsov is starving to death somewhere in the Arctic.

I keep track of Sentsov's hunger strike on my calendar, which I am very attached to because it gives me a sense of knowing. My calendar is on a computer, and it is sunflowerless. It has no idyllic folk scenes, just white pixels and clean lines. Its digital crispness evokes efficiency, minimalism, control. This calendar does not mean to hint at destruction, but I am my grandmother's granddaughter, and so it, too, is a graveyard.

On July 16, 2018, when our airplane left Amsterdam for Lviv, Trump and Putin were still together in Helsinki. Chris and I flew through the night, rainclouds rubbing the windows, and when we entered Ukrainian airspace it was four years to the day since Malaysia Flight 17 was shot from the sky. The war is well into its fifth summer, and it has been, I am told by Ukrainians, a very rainy summer. My calendar is strewn with these confluences, as if by tracking them, I can know them. As if—I am in control.

On the day we go to the village, I know we will take selfies in a sunflower field. What I do not know is that Marina is gone.

+++

Though I do not know it when our van hits the village's jutting cobblestones, Marina has already been dead nine days.

I told you that, Yarosh says. *On the phone. When you called.*
You did?

Yes, he says. Chris and I had been sitting in the center of Lviv, below the city's sweeping Shevchenko monument. I called Yarosh to let him know we were planning a visit. It was a brief and friendly phone call. I hadn't realized anything was wrong. Across the square, Oleg Sentsov's gaunt face hung from a balcony.

I told you, Yarosh says again.

I guess I didn't understand, I say. Yarosh's eyes are blue and shining, and I also want to cry.

We walk again to the cemetery, though this year it is more purposeful. A family of storks watches us from their nest on top of the telephone pole. I remember this same nest from my first visit to the village, over a decade earlier. I wonder if these are their daughter or granddaughter storks. What is the lifespan of a stork? I do not know. On the ground below them, I spot a small clump of leftover poppies.

Marina's grave is still fresh, its soil black and wormy. The mound is covered in ribbons and fabric flowers, yellow, purple, red, white. Someone has left a plate and a spoon for her. It is the ninth day after death, and on the ninth day, we pray the deceased will soon join the nine choirs of heavenly angels. Bohdan, Chris, and Yarosh all stand very stoically, faces serious and squinting in the high sun. Until the 40th day, the dead soul continues to wander, which means Marina is wandering, which means she can still be a messenger, a way of saying hello to those who came before. I cross myself thrice. Please, tell your cousin Busia that I am eating and I am safe. Tell cousin Ivan I am sorry for his suffering. Tell our no-name cousin—if indeed he is there—how he helped save Europe. He is a hero, please tell him that. Tell your uncle Joseph I am sorry for speaking while he could not speak himself. Between two warring empires, he was an impossible man. Tell him I know that. And tell those seven, whoever they are, about our guilt—how I've assumed it because I am alive. Tell them I'm sorry, so so so sorry. It is not fair I am here and they are not. Beg for forgiveness. Holy God, Holy Mighty, Holy Immortal, have mercy on us.

A stork clatters its bill from above. In one ear it sounds like gunfire, in the other, like song.

After crossing myself thrice, I drift back towards the road. I did not expect today would be a day for grief, and I don't know what to do next. The men and I walk quietly for a while. No one seems sure what to say. Goats are feeding in several yards. There is a wafting scent of cow dung, and purple chicory plants stretch from the ditch to touch us. At the village bar, men are laying brick for a new patio. The bricks are rainbow colored. The lady bartender has a look in her eye of amusement, or suspicion, or both. *I remember you from last year,* she says to us.

As we approach the village church, Bohdan breaks the silence by asking Yarosh if it is a Moscow church or a Kyiv church, meaning, does it align with the Ukrainian Orthodox Moscow Patriarchate (a constituent of the Russian Orthodox Church) or the Ukrainian Orthodox Patriarchate based in Kyiv. Critics have called the Moscow church a fifth column, sympathetic to the Kremlin and its dirty war.

It's Russian, Yarosh says.

A pity, Bohdan replies.

Behind the church, there is screaming. Children are jumping from a bridge into the river Ikva below. It is a large crowd, maybe 12 or 15, and they cackle and squeal in the water. When they learn we are Americans, the children want to show us things. One boy begins to perform: front flips, backflips. A girl does the same. Two boys jump together from the blue-and-yellow painted railing. One spreads his arms and legs into a star. Another girl sneaks upstream and floats below where we are perched on the bridge, her tanned chin to the sky, like a surprise otter.

There's a swan family over there, they say, pointing to the sharp reeds.

A very young-looking boy crawls out of the water and sprints toward us holding something prehistoric in his hand. *Crawfish,* he says, pinching the not-quite lizard, not-quite fish. It is alive and flexing. We joke with him about eating it, and he makes a sour face.

Hello! My name is! another boy says, showing off his English from school.

Why are you here? the others ask in Ukrainian. They shout in sing-songy unison.

What are you doing? they ask.

Can we come to America? they ask.

You must study hard, Bohdan tells them. *That is the only way.*

Then the children decide to organize themselves into a line on the grassy bank. It is a big production and takes several minutes to arrange. The swan family watches with skepticism. When the honorary leader of the group says go, the children run and leap, one by one, into the purling Ikva.

+++

Later that same week, I will visit friends in Kyiv. We take the pedestrian bridge from Podil to Trukhaniv Island, a long swatch of green in the middle of the groaning Dnipro. The bridge is busy with lovers and children. A few people are bungee jumping off a wooden platform. An old man in a wool suit plays the fiddle. His hat is full of rainbows. Downriver, the sky swells with a storm. Its clouds are coal-colored and navy, and the wind on the bridge is getting much worse.

I have the distinct feeling, journalist Ivan begins, *that something big is about to happen.*

Like, something personal, or something global? I ask. Ivan has since quit drinking and smoking, and he now bikes 25 miles a day. In terms of lifestyle, it has been a true revolution.

I'm not sure, he says. *But it will be big.*

I feel it, too, standing there, over the hum of the Dnipro, the city's spires in the background, glutted clouds closing in. I wonder if Trump and Putin are plotting right now to carve up the world, Molotov-Ribbentrop style. I wonder if Robert Mueller is in danger. Knock, knock. I wonder if Ivan is, too. I wonder how many more terms Putin will take for himself. Will Poroshenko step down graciously if he loses the next election? Will Trump?

And what will we do, if he doesn't?

But I am getting ahead of myself. That looming sense from the bridge might have its source in something more intimate. Maybe it is a retroactive loom, meant for Marina, or for the sorrow now consuming our Yarosh. He must be very lonely without Marina's keen wit, her large and probing eyes. In the first 40 days, there is a flurry of prayer and ritual and expectation, which keeps one company. There are visitors and meals. After 40 days the loneliness has a chance to settle. It melts downward and inward, like butter to the bone.

But I am getting ahead of myself. Because life is a troika, there is one more bridge to account for. As the village afternoon sinks into evening, we say goodbye to Yarosh again, and head west toward Dubno. Chris and I had made plans to see the town sights—a crumbling military fort and a medieval castle—and spend the night in a B&B full of breakable antiques. The B&B, it turns out, is just a few paces up the road from the prison where Busia's brother Ivan was held and interrogated by the Soviets for seven months. I was not thinking about this particular confluence when we booked the reservation, but it is there nonetheless. I am so well-versed in curating the calendar it seems my subconscious has started to make arrangements on its own. By now I'm convinced our existence begs to be written, an entry composed for each coincidence. I've decided it's my duty to set the uncanny to words, and you would be right to view this impulse with amusement, or suspicion, or both.

After dinner in Dubno, Chris suggests we go for a walk, and though I am exhausted and weepy from this day of unanticipated mourning, I do feel drawn to the river. We take a small footpath from the castle. It is overgrown and buggy. Lady mosquitos swarm our ears, and our ankles itch from Queen Anne's lace. Two stray dogs follow behind. The pups are mangy, stopping every few minutes to gnaw on their knees, but they have kind dog smiles and clearly just want company. The trail spits us out onto a metal bridge slung low over the Ikva. Yes, of course. Surely you knew it would be here, too—the hiccup river. It's chasing us. It runs like we do, through multiple wars, empires, future, present, past, on and on and on, fractaling itself into forever. The river goes where we go.

I expect the river to be here, but what I don't expect is: Chris, down on his knee, a small box in hand, a glint of yellow and blue stone. The dogs sit patiently behind him. On the far bank, where willows hang like curtains, I can see a memorial to those killed on Maidan. It takes me a moment to understand what Chris is asking, but when I do, the answer is obvious.

Perhaps our most absurd human impulse is to try again, to push a rock up a hill, to roll away the boulder week after week. As I write this paragraph, a courtroom in Virginia is announcing that Paul Manafort has been found guilty on eight counts of fraud, while President Donald Trump is calling Manafort a "good man." As I write this paragraph, Oleg Sentsov is on his 100th day of hunger strike. He remains incarcerated in Siberia, held in an empire built on starvation. His heart rate continues to drop.

I have heard that hope is a trap, but what if we choose it, knowingly? Is that not also our agency?

Yes, I tell Chris, which means I am telling my daughter she may go to the revolution. Which means I am telling my granddaughter, too: Yes, of course, leave home and go. I'll be here by the radio, waiting for you.

ACKNOWLEDGMENTS

First, many thanks to Lina María Ferreira Cabeza-Vanegas, for her generous mentorship.

I am grateful to the MFA faculty, administrative staff, and my former classmates at Ohio State who workshopped selections from this book. Thanks especially to Angus Fletcher.

Thanks to *Image* and Seattle Pacific University, for supporting the completion of this project.

Thanks to Kristen Elias Rowley and the entire team at Mad Creek Books, for giving it a good home.

To Shelby, Sean, and Sarah, for giving me a home in which to write it.

To Sam, for every single pep talk.

To Natalia and Maryana, for their expertise.

To Marina and Yaroslav, for their hospitality.

To Mom and John, Mary and Elizabeth, for their endless encouragement.

Special thanks to Tato, for teaching me Ukrainian long before I knew why it mattered, and for bringing me to the village. For showing me the past and future at once.

To Busia and Dido, for feeding us, forever.

And to Chris, for reminding me that "the true revolutionary is guided by great feelings of love." Your insistence made this book possible. I am blessed to call you home.

NOTES

The form and style of "Encyclopedia of Earthly Things" is inspired by Bernardino de Sahagún's "Definitions of Earthly Things," as it appears in *The Lost Origins of the Essay*, edited by John D'Agata and published by Graywolf Press in 2009.

The essay "Duck and Cover" was first published in *Crab Orchard Review*, Vol. 23 No. 1. An earlier version of "Samizdat" appeared in *Colorado Review*, Vol. 43 No. 1. "I Saw the Sunshine, Melting" first appeared in *The Southampton Review*, Vol. 12 No. 1. "Veselka" originally appeared in *Image*, issue 99. It has been reprinted with permission.

WORKS CONSULTED

I am indebted to many scholars and writers who have explored these topics before I did. This is a list, though not exhaustive, of sources that assisted me in thinking about and crafting the essays in this book, and which I recommend for further reading.

Alexievich, Svetlana. *Voices from Chernobyl: The Oral History of a Nuclear Disaster*. Translated by Keith Gessen. Picador, 2006.

Bilocerkowycz, Jaroslaw. *Soviet Ukrainian Dissent: A Study of Political Alienation*. Westview Press, 1988.

Bulgakov, Mikhail. *The Master and Margarita*. Translated by Diana Burgin and Katherine Tiernan O'Connor. Vintage, 1996.

David-Fox, Michael, Peter Holquist, and Alexander M. Martin, editors. *The Holocaust in the East: Local Perpetrators and Soviet Responses*. University of Pittsburgh Press, 2014.

Desbois, Father Patrick. *The Holocaust by Bullets: A Priest's Journey to Uncover the Truth Behind the Murder of 1.5 Million Jews*. St. Martin's Griffin, 2008.

Exeler, Franziska. "The Ambivalent State: Determining Guilt in the Post-World War II Soviet Union." *Slavic Review*. Vol. 75, No. 3 (2016), pp. 606–629.

Gumenyuk, Nataliya. "From a #euromaidan in Ukraine." openDemocracy. 29 November 2013. www.opendemocracy.net/od-russia/nataliya-gumenyuk/from-euromaidan-in-ukraine.

Himka, John-Paul. "Obstacles to the Integration of the Holocaust into Post-Communist East European Historical Narratives." *Canadian Slavonic Papers / Revue Canadienne des Slavistes.* Vol. 50, No. 3/4 (2008), pp. 359–372.

Horvat, Srećko. *The Radicality of Love.* Polity, 2016.

Kellerman, Natan P. F. "Epigenetic Transmission of Holocaust Trauma: Can Nightmares Be Inherited?" *The Israel Journal of Psychiatry and Related Sciences.* Vol. 50, No. 1 (2013), pp. 33–39.

Lower, Wendy. *Nazi Empire-Building and the Holocaust in Ukraine.* University of North Carolina Press, 2007.

Marples, David R. "Stepan Bandera: The Resurrection of a Ukrainian National Hero." *Europe-Asia Studies.* Vol. 58, No. 4 (2006), pp. 555–566.

Miłosz, Czesław. *The Captive Mind.* Translated by Jane Zielonko. Vintage, 1955.

Müller, Herta. *The Land of Green Plums.* Translated by Michael Hoffman. Metropolitan, 2010.

Penter, Tanja. "Collaboration on Trial: New Source Material on Soviet Postwar Trials against Collaborators." *Slavic Review.* Vol. 64, No. 4 (2005), pp. 782–790.

Politkovskaya, Anna. *A Small Corner of Hell: Dispatches from Chechnya.* Translated by Alexander Burry and Tatiana Tulchinksy. University of Chicago Press, 2007.

———. "Poison in the air." *The Guardian.* 1 March 2006. www.theguardian.com/world/2006/mar/01/russia.chechnya.

Rudakova, Daria. "Civilian Collaboration in Occupied Ukraine and Crimea, 1941–1944: A Study of Motivation." PhD Thesis, The University of Western Australia, 2018.

Sereny, Gitta. *Into That Darkness: An Examination of Conscience.* Vintage, 1983.

Shore, Marci. *The Ukrainian Night: An Intimate History of Revolution.* Yale, 2017.

Snyder, Timothy. *Bloodlands: Europe Between Hitler and Stalin.* Basic, 2010.

———. "Germans must remember the truth about Ukraine—for their own sake." *Eurozine.* 7 July 2017. www.eurozine.com/germans-must-remember-the-truth-about-ukraine-for-their-own-sake/.

Solzhenitsyn, Alexandr. *The Gulag Archipelago 1918–1956: An Experiment in Literary Investigation.* Translated by Thomas P. Whitney and Harry Willets. Harper Perennial, 2007.

Subtelny, Orest. *Ukraine: A History.* University of Toronto Press, 1988.

Zhadan, Serhiy. *Depeche Mode.* Translated by Myroslav Shkandrij. Glagoslav, 2013.

21ST CENTURY ESSAYS

David Lazar and Patrick Madden, Series Editors

This series from Mad Creek Books is a vehicle to discover, publish, and promote some of the most daring, ingenious, and artistic nonfiction. This is the first and only major series that announces its focus on the essay—a genre whose plasticity, timelessness, popularity, and centrality to nonfiction writing make it especially important in the field of nonfiction literature. In addition to publishing the most interesting and innovative books of essays by American writers, the series publishes extraordinary international essayists and reprint works by neglected or forgotten essayists, voices that deserve to be heard, revived, and reprised. The series is a major addition to the possibilities of contemporary literary nonfiction, focusing on that central, frequently chimerical, and invariably supple form: The Essay.

Don't Come Back
LINA MARÍA FERREIRA CABEZA-VANEGAS

A Mother's Tale
PHILLIP LOPATE